Linux and the Unix Philosophy

Linux and the Unix Philosophy

Mike Gancarz

Digital Press
An imprint of Elsevier Science

Amsterdam • Boston • Heidelberg • London • New York • Oxford
Paris • San Diego • San Francisco • Singapore • Sydney • Tokyo

Library of Congress Cataloging-in-Publication Data
Gancarz, Mike.
   Linux and the Unix philosophy / Mike Gancarz.
      p. cm.
   Includes bibliographical references and index.
   ISBN: 1-55558-273-7 (pbk. : alk. paper)
   1. Linux.   2. UNIX (Computer file)   3. Operating systems (Computers)
   I. Title.
   QA76.76.O63G364 2003
   005.4'3—dc21   2003051482

British Library Cataloguing-in-Publication Data

A catalogue record for this book is available from the British Library.

The publisher offers special discounts on bulk orders of this book. For information, please contact:

Manager of Special Sales
Elsevier Science
225 Wildwood Avenue
Woburn, MA 01801-2041
Tel: 781-904-2500
Fax: 781-904-2620

For information on all Digital Press publications available, contact our World Wide Web home page at: http://www.bh.com/digitalpress

10 9 8 7 6 5 4 3 2 1

Printed in the United States of America

Every book should have a dedication.
This book is dedicated to the early adopters of Linux everywhere.
You go, gang!

—MG

Contents

Foreword

For me, three major events happened in 1969:

As a student in a major eastern university I had stumbled on a new and fascinating business of writing software for computers. In those days there was no such thing as going down to your local computer store and buying a shrink-wrapped box of software off the shelf. In fact, with the average computer having less than four thousand words of memory, a processor measured in millions of instructions per minute instead of billions of instructions per second, and costing hundreds of thousands of dollars to buy, software was written to make maximum use of the machine's power. Software was written from scratch, with the customer defining the inputs they could supply and the outputs that were desired. The software team (whether in-house or consultants) were then responsible for writing the software that made the transition. If the software did not work, the writers were not paid. Obviously, like any tailor-made item, the software cost a lot of money, but so did the hardware.

Fortunately for me, the Digital Equipment Corporation User Society (DECUS) had a library where people could contribute programs that they had written so that other people could use them. Authors of programs would submit their code to the DECUS library, and the library would then put out a catalog of useful programs, with the cost of copying and mailing by postal mail paid for by the person requesting a copy of the program. The software was free, the distribution (and the costs of printing the catalog, etc.) were not.

Through DECUS I got a lot of free software that I could use. This was good, since as a student I did not have much money to buy tailored software. It was either the software or beer, and the five dollars I would spend in 1969 for copying a text editor would be equivalent to ten pitchers of beer. Imagine how thin I would have been to try and purchase "commercial" software.

Why did these people contribute the software they had written? They had written the software because they needed it for their own work or research, and they (graciously) thought that perhaps someone else might be able to use it also. They also (rightly) hoped that others might help them improve it, or at least give them ideas for improvement.

The second major event of 1969 was that Ken Thompson, Dennis Ritchie and a few other researchers at AT&T Bell Laboratories in New Jersey started writing an operating system that eventually became known as "UNIX". As they wrote it, they formed a methodology that the operating system should be made up of small, re-usable components rather than large, monolithic programs. In addition, they developed an architecture for an operating system that would allow it to be portable, and eventually run on the smallest of embedded devices to the largest of supercomputers, no matter what the instruction set of the main CPU looked like. Eventually this operating system escaped to universities and then to corporate America, where it was used mostly on server machines.

The third major event, one that would change my life and the life of millions of other people in a significant way, but at the time hardly noticed by anyone other than two proud parents in Helsinki, was the birth of Linus Torvalds, who was later to become the architect of the Linux kernel.

Over the next ten years computer science moved at a steady pace. Companies invested in new software and techniques. As each company reached further with what they were doing with computers, they followed the technique of purchasing tailor-made software to work on those computers that were still (by today's standards) impossibly small, impossibly slow and impossibly expensive. Yet the people at AT&T working on Unix and the universities that were helping them continued to do their work in creating an operating system that encouraged the re-use of software, and traded off the possibility of more efficient code for the efficiency in not having to re-write and re-invent the wheel. Universities and computer science researchers liked having the source code for the operating system so they could collaborate on making it better. Life was good.

Then in the early 1980s three major events again happened.

The first was the commercialization of Unix. By this time the cost of minicomputers had dropped to the point where the costs of programming and training of users were beginning to overcome the costs of the basic hardware. Sun Microsystems created a market where various customers were demanding an "Open System", which ran on many processor types, rather than the current "proprietary" systems such as MVS, MPE, VMS, and the other commercial operating systems. Companies such as Digital Equipment Corporation, IBM and Hewlett Packard began to think about creating a "commercial" version of Unix for themselves. In order to protect their investments, and to get a lower royalty price from AT&T, they put out a binary-only distribution. The source code for Unix systems was placed at such a high price that few could afford it. Wholesale sharing of the improvements to Unix came to a halt.

The second event was the advent of the microprocessor. At first this created an atmosphere of software sharing through bulletin boards, magazines and computer clubs. However a new concept came about, that of "shrink-wrapped" software. Software written to "commodity" processor architectures such as Intel or Motorola, with hardware produced in the hundreds and thousands of units. Initially with CP/M, then later with MSDOS and Apple's OS, the number of shrink-wrapped products increased. I still remember walking into my first computer store and seeing lots of computers from different companies and of different hardware architectures on the shelf, but only three or four software products (a word processor, a spreadsheet, some type of "modem software"). Of course none of these had the source code with them. If you could not get them to work with the software and documentation you had with them, you were stuck. Open collaboration in writing software was slowly replaced by binary-only code, end-user licenses (telling you how you should use the software you bought), software patents and eternal copyrights.

Fortunately back in those days the number of customers for each company was still small. You might even get some help when you called their support line. But trying to build on top of what these companies had done was close to impossible.

The third event was actually a result of the first two. At a small office in MIT, a researcher named Richard Stallman decided that he liked hacking on the source code to Unix and other software packages. He hated the ever-decreasing exposure to source code he had, and decided to start a project in 1984 to write a complete operating system that would forever have its source code available to people. As a side-effect of having freely distributable sources, the software would forever be free of cost for people who wished to pull down the source code and compile their own operating system. He called this project "GNU" for "GNU is Not Unix", to show his displeasure for having the sources of Unix taken away from him.

Time marched on. Microsoft became a dominant force in the operating system business, with other system vendors bringing out various versions of Unix, most of which were incompatible with each other in the name of "innovation". A whole market of shrink-wrapped, inflexible software emerged, each packaged program written for a commodity market that needed unique solutions.

Then around 1990 three more events happened:

The first was that a small group of Unix professionals were sitting around a table comparing the different types of software in different markets and one of them asked (and it may have been me):

"Why do you like Unix?"

Most of the people at the table did not know what to answer at first, but as the question lingered in the air each of them started to give their reason for liking the operating system to which they had such fierce loyalty. Issues such as "re-use of code", "efficient, well-written utilities", "simple, yet elegant" were mentioned and expanded as reasons. None of us noticed that one person was writing down these ideas as we brought them out. Those ideas became the core for the first edition of this book, and it was the first time that someone had written a "philosophy book" about Unix.

Why was a book on the "Philosophy of Unix" needed? To help first-time Unix users to understand the true power and elegance of the system. To show them that a little thought in writing programs using the tools and structures of Unix could save them significant amounts of time and effort. To help them extend the system, not work against it. To help them stand on the shoulders of those who had gone before.

Secondly, by 1990, a lot of the GNU project had been written. Command interpreters, utilities, compilers, libraries, and more. These pieces of the GNU project, in conjunction with other pieces of freely available software such as sendmail, BIND, and the X Window System were only missing the core part of the operating system called the "kernel".

The kernel was the brains of the system, the thing that controlled the time that programs ran, what memory they were given, what files they had access to and other things. It had been left to last because kernels were changing day to day and improving all the time. Having a kernel with no utilities or command interpreters would not have been useful. Having all the tools available for use on other operating systems and other kernels had been very useful over the years.

Third, in December of 1990 Linus Torvalds had grown to be a university student at the University of Helsinki, and he had just gotten a new Intel 386 computer. Linus recognized that the Microsoft operating system of that time did not take advantage of all of the power of the 386, and he was determined to write a kernel, and mate it with the rest of the freely available software available to create an entire operating system. Almost as an afterthought he determined that the kernel should be licensed by the General Public License of the GNU project. He announced the project to some newsgroups on the Internet, and work commenced.

In April of 1994 I watched while Kurt Reisler, chairman of the Unix Special Interest Group (SIG) of DECUS tried to gather funds to have a programmer come to the United States to talk to the DECUS SIG about the project he was working on. Eventually I asked my management at Digital to fund this effort, mostly on the faith that Kurt usually had good insight into things. In May of 1994 I attended the DECUS event in New Orleans, met Linus Torvalds, saw the operating system for the first time and my life was changed forever.

In the past years I have spent advocating a re-implementation of the Unix operating system I loved so much, but in a way that encouraged people to look at, modify and improve the source code that others had built before them. Actually it has grown much beyond what most people would think of as "Unix", since the free software movement now includes databases, multimedia software, business software and other software valuable to millions of people.

Once again the tide of software production had changed. Hardware had become so sophisticated and so cheap, collaboration on the Internet so easy, and the speed of software information so fast that at long last major groups could come together to develop software that helped them solve their own problems. No longer did software have to be done in lofty "cathedrals", using expensive machinery, created by self-proclaimed druids of architecture. Cries of "here is the code" came from people who now had the means to make major contributions to computer science from their homes and classrooms, whether that was in the United States, Brazil, China, or "even" Helsinki, Finland. Tens of thousands of projects started, with hundreds of thousands of programmers helping, and it keeps expanding at an ever-increasing speed.

The future of computer programming will not be the small group of huddled programmers trying futilely to create code that matches 100% of everyone's needs. Instead large groups of software will exist on the net in source code form, begging for consultants and value-added resellers to pull it down and create a *solution* for the customer by tailoring this code *exactly* to their customer's needs.

So you see, the concept of Linux and the GNU project while appearing to be the "next step" of the Unix Philosophy is only the return from a wayward path. Everything stated in the Unix Philosophy's first edition is just as true today, perhaps even more so. The addition of source code availability allows you to see exactly how these masters of code created their systems, and challenges you to create even faster code with greater capabilities.

May you stand on the shoulders of giants, and touch the stars.

Carpe Diem,

Jon "maddog" Hall
Executive Director
Linux International

Acknowledgments

The birth of a book is like the birth of a child: every one is different. The writing and publication of my first book, *The UNIX Philosophy*, had gone fairly smoothly as books go. Had I known that I would have faced so much personal turmoil during the writing of this second book, I would not likely have signed the publishing contract. I would have thought twice before getting involved in this project.

Having endured the personal turmoil amidst the writing and publishing process, I admit that this book is a sort of catharsis then, both personally and philosophically. So I must give credit to the great God Almighty for getting me through this process once again. He first and foremost deserves the credit for creating me to do such a work as this.

Kudos go to Pam Chester, acquisitions editor at Digital Press, an imprint of Butterworth-Heinemann, for selling me on the need to do this new edition and then persevering when it had every appearance of becoming another pre-publication casualty. Thanks also go to her boss, Theron Shreve, for having the patience to allow the book to come to its full fruition.

I was fortunate to have an awesome crew of developmental reviewers for this edition. Thanks go to Jim Lieb, Scott Morris, Rob Lembree, and Jes Sorensen for their thoughtful insights. Their responses helped me see things in different ways and added much interesting depth to the book. They also provided much-needed encouragement on the home stretch.

Not only does Jon "maddog" Hall deserve special mention for providing an insightful foreword to this book, his efforts at Unix and Linux advocacy are a model for all of us. Few can match his tireless efforts at bringing the message of the Unix way to so many people.

Thanks also go to Phil Sutherland, formerly of Digital Press, for the email exchanges we'd had on the original book idea. Even though it didn't turn out quite the way that either of us expected, he can take heart that his efforts to convince me to write this were not in vain. Some things just take a little longer than others.

Having an author in a household means that everyone learns what it's like to live with a writer. Thank you, Sarah, for all that typing, as boring as it must have been for you. Adam, it's paintball time. I am deeply grateful for the sacrifice you made. And, most importantly, thanks go to my wife Viv for supporting me throughout the writing of this book. Your "Honey-Do" list must be a mile long by now.

Preface

Several years after the publication of *The UNIX Philosophy*[1], Phil Sutherland, formerly the publisher at Digital Press, approached me about writing a book on Linux. He said that Linux was going to be big and that he believed that there was a need for a "Linux philosophy" sort of book. Phil and I proceeded to discuss the topic at great length in a series of email exchanges that lasted more than a year. And, despite the established need for such a book and the wealth of ideas to fill it, something just wasn't right about it.

Phil was pushing for a Linux edition of *The UNIX Philosophy*, which certainly would have made sense from a marketing perspective. But I was seeing something different going on in the Linux community. There was a fresh vigor flowing through the Unix world. It was clear that the aging Unix devotees had succeeded in infusing knowledge of the "way of thinking that is Unix" into the minds of a new, vibrant breed of hackers and other enthusiasts who loved to play with the insides of Unix *on their own machines*. Linux is Unix, yes, but it's not your father's Unix.

I'd wanted to capture this spirit of innovation in a book that was to be titled "The Linux Manifesto". Eventually it became apparent that "open source" was what Linux really was about. So "The Linux Manifesto" would have to be renamed "The Open Source Manifesto" if it were to fit the subject matter. But Eric Raymond had already written the best "this is why we do this" piece about open source in his classic *The Cathedral and the Bazaar*[2]. I wasn't keen about doing a copycat book and so the idea was shelved for a time.

---

1. Gancarz, Mike, *The UNIX Philosophy*, Digital Press, 1995.

2. Raymond, Eric S., *The Cathedral and the Bazaar: Musings on Linux and Open Source by an Accidental Revolutionary*. Sebastopol, CA: O'Reilly & Associates, Inc., 2001.

Good ideas have a tendency to come back in a different form when the original idea doesn't pan out. Pam Chester of Digital Press pointed out to me a couple of years ago that some of the information in *The UNIX Philosophy* had become dated and asked if I would be interested in doing a revision. But how does one revise a philosophy? If something is The Truth, then it will continue to be The Truth a month from now, a year from now, and even centuries from now.

Then it finally dawned on me. *The UNIX Philosophy* book, as a description of the Unix way of thinking, was a "first system". It was now being drawn into becoming a "second system". And the second system, in this case, is a fuller, more developed, more relevant edition of the first. While *The UNIX Philosophy* was the bare necessities, *Linux and the Unix Philosophy* takes the original concepts forward and explores new territory. It also still retains the original philosophical tenets because The Truth is still The Truth.

So the readers of the first book are going to find plenty of familiar ideas here. The original tenets of the Unix philosophy are still intact, but I've gone over every chapter to examine how to best express things in a Linux context. In one sense, this book is a revision of the first. But in another it is exploring new ground. The developmental reviewers have spoken of this in their feedback. It has helped them to look at Unix in ways that the first book never did. It is one thing to tell people that the Unix philosophy has affected how Unix programmers have written an operating system. It is a bolder proposition to show how the philosophy is having an effect on other parts of the computer world and even life outside of the computer world.

The software world is undergoing a major shift once again because of Linux and open source software. The Unix philosophy is going mainstream in the computer industry now. Lots of people have adopted its tenets. These ideas have caused a dramatic upheaval as icons are cast aside and people are questioning whether there is a different way to embrace computing on a personal level. Linux is right there, standing in this gap, offering a way for mainstream computer users to experience Unix first-hand. As more of them experience Linux, they are seeing what they perceive as new ways of doing things. The Unix devotees, on the other hand, are finding that personal computing is coming back to familiar territory.

The Linux philosophy is really the Unix philosophy on steroids. I say this emphatically and in conflict with those who would choose to believe that Linux is not Unix. But I am also quick to admit that Linux as a phenomenon is different from what has transpired with Unix. The Linux community is much more attuned to overcoming proprietary approaches to software development than the Unix community ever realized that it had to be.

The Linux community is more savvy, market-wise, too. It recognizes that for Linux to win, it must outthink, outplay, and outspin the competition at every turn. It's doing an outstanding job. The Linux developers, rumored to be more than a million, are vociferously challenging the works of the other operating system developers on their own turf in every vital area: ease of installation, graphical user interface, hardware compatibility, reliability, security, performance, web development, databases, games, and so on.

Thanks to the persistent efforts of its development community, Linux has become the proverbial itch that doesn't go away no matter how much you scratch it.

Who will benefit from this book

In the early days, only system programmers found Unix material interesting. Today's Linux users and developers comprise a far more diverse group with a variety of personal and professional interests. As Linux moves towards the computing mainstream, the kind of people who had never heard about Unix before have seen, used, and perhaps even own a Linux system. In this book I have tried to reach many of them by avoiding low-level technical details while providing thought-provoking views of the nature of Unix, Linux, and open source software. These fringe people will find in here an introduction to Unix ideas and the realization of them in Linux without getting bogged down in command parameters, programmatic interfaces, and such.

Linux developers will benefit from learning the cornerstone ideas of Unix contained here and how Linux has embraced and enhanced them. They will learn that, while Linux has an excellent graphical user interface environment, its intrinsic worth comes from the philosophy behind it. In order to become a true Linux "power user", they need to understand why its textual under- pinnings and tools approach give it overwhelming advantages over the competition.

"Old school" Unix programmers might consider reading this book because it will help them to realize why Unix has not gone away and why it will never go away. In Linux, it has simply reinvented itself in a new, more capable form. This book will show them how Linux addresses the computing needs of the new millennium in new, exciting ways while preserving the tenets of the original Unix philosophy.

Other seasoned developers working in today's fast-paced, highly competitive development environments often find that there is great pressure to abscond with the principles of good software design. In other cases, companies put great emphasis on using new development processes because they are the latest fads instead of ensuring that their approaches have sufficient substance. This book serves as a kind of sanity check when design issues appear impossible to resolve or solutions contain questionable assumptions.

In the business world, IT managers today already know about Linux. Many are considering introducing it into their environments because of anticipated cost savings. Their strategy is usually one of replacing older Solaris and HP-UX platforms with less expensive Intel- or AMD-based Linux servers for the less critical applications. As IBM and Oracle further enhance their Linux offerings, switching to Linux for their primary servers will be a more acceptable option than it was a few years ago.

However, IT managers thus far have been afraid to migrate their desktop users to Linux. This book will help them to realize that, not only is Linux a viable alternative, it is actually the *preferred* alternative. They will find that the philosophy behind Linux and open source software actually makes desktops easier to maintain, less costly, and more secure than their Windows-based counterparts. The same ideas that make Linux an ideal server also carry forth to the desktop. Before they respond with "Yes, but…", I have one thing to say to them: Read the book.

Finally, people who deal with the abstract world of ideas will find value in learning about the Unix philosophy. Many techniques used to develop software apply to other endeavors as well. Writers, graphic artists, teachers, and speakers may discover that rapid prototyping and leveraging work in their fields, too. And with the plethora of inexpensive (as in "free") Linux applications available today, they can afford to use the kinds of tools that were formerly too costly for them to explore.

Chapter overviews

Chapter 1—"The Unix Philosophy: A Cast of Thousands" explores the history of the Unix philosophy and how it came about. It also briefly describes the tenets of the Unix philosophy as a prelude to the longer explanations provided in subsequent chapters.

Chapter 2—"One Small Step for Humankind" shows why small components are best for building large systems. It discusses their ability to interface well with each other, both in software systems and in the physical world. The last part of the chapter focuses on the importance of having programs that do one thing well.

Chapter 3—"Rapid Prototyping for Fun and Profit" stresses the necessity of constructing prototypes early when designing a successful product. A discussion of the Three Systems of Man illustrates the phases that all software passes through. It defends rapid prototyping as the fastest route to the Third System, the most correct of the three.

Chapter 4—"The Portability Priority" provides a different perspective on software portability. It emphasizes that software developers must choose between efficiency and portability in their designs. The Atari VCS is studied as a model of high efficiency and limited portability. The chapter also highlights data portability as an important, though often overlooked, goal. A case study of the typical Unix user's collection of tools provides an excellent example of software longevity due to portability.

Chapter 5—"Now That's Leverage!" discusses the idea of "software leverage," where reusing components results in greater impact. We see how the use of shell scripts achieves a high degree of leverage.

Chapter 6—"The Perils of Interactive Programs" begins by defining Captive User Interfaces. It suggests that developers limit their usage and instead focus on making programs interact better with other programs. It expresses the idea that all programs are filters. The chapter ends with a discussion of filters in the Unix environment.

Chapter 7—"More Unix Philosophy: Ten Lesser Tenets" lists several notions that Unix developers generally follow but don't consider primary elements of the Unix philosophy. Since this chapter deals with some concepts at deeper levels than the rest of the book, the less technical reader should feel free to skip this chapter. Unix purists, however, will likely find it quite entertaining.

Chapter 8—"Making Unix Do One Thing Well" presents the Unix mail handler MH as an example of how good Unix applications are built. It finishes with a summary of the Unix philosophy that shows how it derives its strength from each element working together.

Chapter 9—"Unix and Other Operating System Philosophies" compares Linux and the Unix philosophy to several other operating system philosophies to emphasize the uniqueness of the Unix approach.

Chapter 10—"Through the Glass Darkly: Linux vs. Windows" starts with a high-level comparison between Linux and Microsoft Windows. It makes the case for text-based computing versus the use of graphical user interfaces. It then wraps up with a look at how Windows adheres to the Unix philosophy in some areas and departs from it in others.

Chapter 11—"A Cathedral? How Bizarre!" takes a look at how the concept of Open Source Software (OSS) popularized by the Linux community fits with the Unix philosophy. The propagation of OSS works best when it employs the "Unix way of thinking" in all areas.

Chapter 12—"Brave New (Unix) World" examines how the tenets of the Unix philosophy are being adopted in new technological areas. It focuses on several key and a few not-so-key technologies to illustrate that Unix ideas are not just for Unix developers anymore. This book's developmental reviewers' most frequent comment about Chapter 12 was "I never thought of it that way before." Read it and it will open your mind.

As you've probably already seen from a quick glance, the text avoids many technical details as they vary from one Linux implementation to another. Instead, it stresses that the Unix philosophy is a design methodology that depends less on specifics and more on a general approach defined at a higher level.

I've tried to keep an upbeat tone throughout the book. While some people may enjoy reading massive technical tomes lacking humanity, the rest of us prefer writing that is both entertaining and informative, i.e., the "infotainment" approach. This, too, is in keeping with the Linux and Unix culture. The Unix community and its offspring Linux community has always had a wry sense of humor. It shows in places in the original Bell Laboratories' Unix documents and on the networks frequented by Linux people. Perhaps it's why Linux developers enjoy their work so much.

Do not be dissuaded by the levity, however. This is serious stuff. People have found or lost software fortunes by observing or ignoring the tenets covered here. Proper applications of the Unix philosophy have usually resulted in tremendously successful products. Operating in direct conflict with these tenets has often caused developers to miss important windows of market opportunity.

Students of my lectures have mentioned that, while you may at first superficially absorb ideas expressed here, they return to your conscious mind at odd times. Powerful ideas tend to do that. If you have never been exposed to the Unix philosophy before, prepare yourself for an interesting journey.

The introduction to the original Unix philosophy book is included here for a couple of reasons. The first is that people have immortalized it by quoting from it on the Internet. Keeping it in this edition will enable those people who have not purchased the original book to benefit from it. The second reason is because of the prophetic statement in the last paragraph: "…it is only a matter of time before Unix becomes the world's operating system." Linux, as the new namesake of Unix, is fulfilling that statement day by day, machine by machine, application by application.

Introduction to The Unix Philosophy

An operating system is a living, breathing software entity. The soul of the computing machine, it is the nervous system that turns electrons and silicon into a personality. It brings life to the computer.

An operating system, by its nature, embodies the philosophy of its creators. The Apple Mac/OS, with its highly visual, object-oriented user interface, proclaims "it's right there in front of you." Microsoft's MS-DOS, the undisputed leader of the personal computer revolution, tries to bring "a taste of the mainframe" to the desktop. Digital Equipment Corporation's OpenVMS assumes that the user fears the electronic thinking machine and must be given only a few powerful choices to accomplish a task.

The creators of the Unix operating system started with a radical concept: They assumed that the user of their software would be computer literate from the start. The entire Unix philosophy revolves around the idea that the user knows what he is doing. While other operating system designers take great pains to accommodate the breadth of users from novice to expert, the designers of Unix took an inhospitable "if you can't understand it, you don't belong here" kind of approach.

It was precisely this attitude that prevented Unix from gaining wide acceptance early. It was confined to the back room where academics studied it because of the intoxicating fumes it brought to the ivory towers ("The parallels one can draw between the Unix file system hierarchy and the natural order of things bears careful intellectual scrutiny") and "techies" tinkered with it because it gave them more ways to play than any other system before it.

Alas, the commercial world could see no value in it. It was a hacker's toy, a curiosity. Few profitable enterprises would dare risk their investment returns on an operating system that came from a research lab, was nurtured in universities, and was self-supported by the purchaser. As a result, Unix languished for more than 15 years as an unsung hero.

Then an amazing thing happened in the early 1980's. Rumors began to circulate that there was an operating system that provided more flexibility, more portability, and more capability than whatever it was that people where currently using. Furthermore, it was universally available at very little cost and it could run on just about anyone's machine.

The message of Unix sounded nearly too good to be true, but history has a way of proving that we often shoot the messenger. Whenever any radical idea comes along that seriously alters our view of the world, our natural tendency is to bash the bearer of new tidings. As far as anyone in the computing mainstream could see, these "Unix fanatics" were not interested in evolution - they were talking revolution.

As Unix began to infiltrate the computing world, evidently many in today's corporate bureaucracies abhorred the thought of revolution. They preferred their ordered world on PC's and mainframes, secure in the belief that job security came from knowing the simple commands that they'd struggled to learn and use in their daily tasks. Unix became The Enemy, not so much because it was intrinsically evil, but because it threatened the status quo.

For years Unix pioneers lived in relative obscurity. Support for their radical ideas was nowhere to be found. Even when some sympathetic soul would listen to the tirades of the local Unix advocate, the response would usually be "Unix is okay, but if you want to do anything serious, you should probably use _____." (Fill the blank with the name of your favorite mainstream operating system.) Still, operating system philosophies are like religions. When someone has it in their head that they have found The Truth, they're not willing to let it go that easily. So the Unix apostles pressed on, doggedly upholding the standard, believing that someday the world would be converted and they would see software paradise.

While the commercial world was busy building barriers to Unix, the academic world was welcoming Unix with open arms. A generation of young people raised in houses with color TV's, microwave ovens, and video games was entering universities that had obtained Unix for the cost of the magnetic media on which it was distributed. These young people had clean canvases for minds and the professors were more than willing to paint on them a picture of computing far removed from the mainstream.

The rest is history.

Today Unix is rapidly gaining acceptance in situations where it once would have been considered unthinkable. It is the undisputed system of choice in the academic world, and its applications in the military and commercial worlds are expanding daily.

I have been telling people for years that it is only a matter of time before Unix becomes the world's operating system. I have yet to be proven wrong. Ironically, however, the world's operating system will not be called "Unix," for as companies have realized the value of the name, their lawyers have rushed to register its trademark. As a result, interfaces will be designed, standards will be proposed, and many applications will be written in the name of "open systems." Rest assured, though, that the Unix philosophy will be the driving force behind them all.

The Unix Philosophy: A Cast of Thousands

The philosophy of one century is the common sense of the next.
Chinese fortune cookie

Many people credit Ken Thompson of AT&T with inventing the Unix operating system and, in a sense, they're right. Thompson wrote the first Unix version in 1969 at AT&T's Research Division of Bell Laboratories in Murray Hill, New Jersey. It ran on a Digital PDP-7 minicomputer as a platform for the program Space Travel. Space Travel originally ran on the Multics system, developed at the Massachusetts Institute of Technology.

Unix is based on Multics, one of the first timesharing operating systems. Before the development of Multics, most computer operating systems operated in batch mode, forcing programmers to edit large stacks of punched cards or paper tape. Programming in those days was a very time-consuming process. It was a period when the saying "Heaven help the twit who drops his box of punch cards" was readily understood by all.

Thompson borrowed many features of Multics and included them in his early versions of Unix, the principal characteristic being that of timesharing. Without this capability, most of the features taken for granted in today's Unix systems—and in most other operating systems for that matter—would lack real power.

By borrowing ideas from Multics, Thompson embarked upon a course of action that has become a well-worn path (no pun intended) for Unix developers: Good programmers write great software; great programmers "steal" great software. No, we're not implying that Thompson was a thief. But his willingness to avoid the "not invented here" (NIH) syndrome in some respects and yet add creative value in some others helped launch possibly the most ingenious operating system in history. We'll explore the significance of "stealing" software later. For now, bear in mind that an idea shared is worth two kept in the brain.

1.1   The Not invented here syndrome

All too often software developers fall prey to the NIH syndrome. This occurs when a developer, in viewing a software solution written by another, believes that he or she could do a better job. Maybe he could do a better job, but he doesn't know the constraints that the other developer was operating under. The other may have been under time or budget pressure and chose to focus more on a particular part of the solution.

NIH syndrome is characterized by a decision to discard all of what the other developer accomplished with the intent of demonstrating a superior solution. Such an act of sheer egotism demonstrates little interest in preserving the best of another's work and using it as a springboard to newer heights. Not only is it self-serving, it wastes precious time on rewriting, time that would be better be spent elsewhere on providing other solutions. Even worse, the new solution is sometimes only marginally better or simply different, thereby exacerbating the problem.

Occasionally, the new solution is better because the developer has seen the work of the first and is able to improve upon it by borrowing what is good and discarding the rest. That is a case of enhancement and extension, not the NIH syndrome. The concept of borrowing from other developers is a well-established practice in the Linux world, something that can be done only when software source code is made available to everyone. In fact, enhancement and extension constitute one of the core concepts of the Unix philosophy.

1.2   Developing Unix

People marvel at the portability of Unix, but it wasn't always portable. Thompson originally coded it in assembly language. In 1972 he rewrote it in a portable language called B as it became evident that he might want to take advantage of new hardware as it became available. Another member of AT&T's staff at Bell Laboratories, Dennis Ritchie, made extensive modifications to B in 1973, evolving it into the C language loved and despised today by programmers the world over.

Again, Thompson had set a precedent that was later adopted by Unix developers: Someone whose back is against the wall often writes great programs. When an application must be written, and (1) it must be done to meet a practical need, (2) there aren't any "experts" around who would know how to write it, and (3) there is no time to do it "right," the odds are very good that an outstanding piece of software will be written. In Thompson's case, he needed an operating system written in a portable language because he had to move his programs from one hardware architecture to another. No self-described portable operating system experts could be found. And he certainly didn't have time to do it "right."

Ken Thompson played a limited role in the development of the overall Unix philosophy, however. Although he made significant design contributions in the areas of file system structure, pipes, the I/O subsystem, and portability, much of the Unix philosophy came about as a result of many peoples' efforts. Each person who worked with Unix in its early days helped to shape it according to his or her area of expertise. The following lists some contributors and their primary contributions:

Contributors	Contributions
Alfred Aho	Text scanning, parsing, sorting
Eric Allman	Electronic mail
Kenneth Arnold	Screen updating
Stephen Bourne	Bourne shell command interpreter
Lorinda Cherry	Interactive calculator
Steven Feldman	Computer-aided software engineering
Stephen Johnson	Compiler design tools
William Joy	Text editing, C-like command language
Brian Kernighan	Regular expressions, programming principles, typesetting, computer-aided instruction
Michael Lesk	High-level text formatting, dial-up networking
John Mashey	Command interpreter
Robert Morris	Desk calculator
D. A. Nowitz	Dial-up networking
Joseph Ossanna	Text formatting language
Dennis Ritchie	C programming language
Larry Wall	Patch utility, Perl command language, *rn* network news reader
Peter Weinberger	Text scanning

Although the above individuals are the earliest and most recognizable participants in the Unix phenomenon, the people who developed the Unix approach to computing eventually numbered in the thousands. Virtually every published paper on a major Unix component lists more than a handful of contributors who helped make it happen. These contributors formed the Unix philosophy as it is understood and propagated today.

1.3   Linux: A cast of one plus one million

If it can be said that Ken Thompson is the inventor of Unix, then Linus Torvalds, at the time a Finnish student at the University of Helsinki, invented Linux. His now famous newsgroup posting on August 25, 1991, that began with "Hello everybody out there.... I'm doing a (free) operating system" sealed his fate forever.

The similarities between Thompson and Torvalds are curious, to say the least. One could argue that Thompson wrote the program Space Travel just for the fun of it. Torvalds, in his fascination with Minix, another Unix-like operating system, found it all too interesting to make a version of a popular Unix command interpreter, *bash*, run on his "toy" operating system. Again, what started out as "for fun" ended up changing fundamental aspects of the software industry.

Linux didn't start out as a portable operating system either. Torvalds had no intentions of porting it beyond the Intel 386 architecture. In one sense, his back was against the wall, because he had only a minimal amount of computer hardware available to him. So he made the most of what he had without intending to take it any further in the beginning. He found, though, that good design principles and a solid development model eventually led him to make Linux more portable for purity's sake alone. Others carried the ball from that point and ported it to other architectures soon afterward.

By the time Torvalds's Linux came along, the idea of borrowing software written by other individuals had become fairly commonplace. So much so, in fact, that Richard M. Stallman formalized it in his landmark GNU Public License. The GPL is a legal agreement applied to software that virtually guarantees that the source code to the software remains freely available to anyone who wants it. Torvalds eventually adopted the GPL scheme for Linux and, by doing so, made it possible for anyone to borrow the Linux source code without fear of legal entanglements associated with copyright infringement.[1] Since Torvalds was giving away Linux for free, it was only natural that others would contribute their software gratis to the Linux development efforts.

From its early days, Linux had already exhibited that it was indeed a Unix-like operating system. Its developers embraced the tenets of the Unix philosophy wholeheartedly, then went on to write a new operating system from scratch. The catch is, almost nothing in the Linux world is written from scratch anymore. Nearly everything is built on top of code and concepts writ-

---

1.   Torvalds borrowed much more than the GPL. Stallman and others have pointed out that Linux is really the operating system kernel. Much of everything outside the kernel comes from the Free Software Foundation's GNU Project. The purists rightfully call the complete system "GNU/Linux," of which the Linux kernel is an essential component. Having given credit where credit is due, we recognize that most of the world has already recognized "Linux" as the nomenclature of choice.

ten by others. So Linux became the natural next step in the evolution of Unix or, perhaps more accurately, the next big leap for Unix.

Like Unix, Linux has its share of developers who helped it along in the early stages of its technical development. But whereas the number of Unix developers at its peak numbered in the thousands, the number of Linux developers today is in the millions. Talk about extreme Unix! It is this massive scale of development that virtually guarantees that Unix's descendant Linux will be a system to contend with for a long time to come.

A new wrinkle that Linux brought to the Unix world is the idea that so-called "open source" software is better than "proprietary" software or software for which the source code isn't readily available. Unix developers have believed that for years, but the rest of the people in the computer industry were being fed lots of propaganda by proprietary software companies that anything borrowed or free cannot be as good as something for which one has to pay money—sometimes huge amounts of money.

The Linux community is more savvy about marketing too, having learned that companies can successfully sell inferior software to millions if it is marketed well. This is not to say that Linux is inferior software, only that, unlike its Unix community predecessor, the Linux community recognizes that even the best software in the world will not be used unless people know about it and realize its true worth.

We will be covering these topics in more depth later. For now, let us leave the history of Unix and Linux in the past and move on. Things are about to get much more interesting.

1.4   The Unix philosophy in a nutshell

The tenets of the Unix philosophy are deceptively simple. They are so simple, in fact, that people tend to regard them as having little importance. That's where the deception comes in. Their simplicity disguises the fact that these ideas are incredibly effective when carried out consistently.

The following list will give you an idea of *what* the Unix philosophy tenets are. The rest of the book will help you to understand *why* they are important.

1.   *Small is beautiful.* Small things have tremendous advantages over their larger counterparts. Among these is the ability to combine

with other small things in unique and useful ways, ways often unforeseen by the original designer.

2.   *Make each program do one thing well.* By focusing on a single task, a program can eliminate much extraneous code that often results in excess overhead, unnecessary complexity, and a lack of flexibility.

3.   *Build a prototype as soon as possible.* Most people would agree that prototyping is a valuable element of any project. But whereas prototyping is only a small part of the design phase under other methodologies, under Unix it is the principal vehicle for generating an effective design.

4.   *Choose portability over efficiency.* When Unix broke new ground as the first portable operating system of any significance, it was big news. Today portability is taken for granted as a necessity in any modern software design, an example of a tenet that has gained wide acceptance on other systems besides Unix.

5.   *Store data in flat text files.* The choice between portability and efficiency addresses the value of portable code. Portable data is at least as important as—if not more important than—portable code. Portable data is the often-neglected part of the portability formula.

6.   *Use software leverage to your advantage.* Many programmers have only a superficial understanding of the importance of reusable code modules. Code reuse helps one take advantage of software leverage, a powerful concept that some Unix developers use to create numerous applications in a comparatively short time.

7.   *Use shell scripts to increase leverage and portability.* Shell scripts are double-edged swords for enhancing both software leverage and portability in a design. Whenever possible, writing a script instead of a complete C program is the way to go.

8.   *Avoid captive user interfaces.* Some commands have user interfaces known to Unix developers as "captive" user interfaces. These prevent the user from running other commands while the command is in use, effectively making the user a captive to the system for the duration of the command. In a graphical user interface world, such interfaces would be called "modal."

9.   *Make every program a filter.* The fundamental nature of all software programs is that they only modify data; they do not create it. Therefore, they should be written to perform as filters since they *are* filters.

The preceding list contains tenets about which Unix developers are dogmatic. You will find similar lists in other books on Unix, as they are the points that everyone considers to be foundational Unix concepts. If you adopt them, you will be considered to be a "Unix person."

The following lists 10 lesser tenets, ideas that tend to be part of the Unix world's belief system.[2] Not everyone involved with Unix is dogmatic about these, and some of them aren't strictly characteristic of Unix. Still, they seem to be a part of the Unix culture (and the Linux culture by inclusion).

1. *Allow the user to tailor the environment.* Unix users like the ability to control their environment—all of it. Many Unix applications decidedly refrain from making decisions about styles of interaction and instead leave the choices to the user. The idea here is to implement mechanisms for doing things, not policies for how to do them. Let users discover their own paths to computer nirvana.

2. *Make operating system kernels small and lightweight.* Despite the never-ending push for new features, Unix developers prefer to keep the most central part of an operating system small. They don't always succeed at this, but this is their goal.

3. *Use lowercase and keep it short.* Using lowercase characters is a tradition in the Unix environment that has persisted long after the reason for doing so disappeared. Many Unix users today use lowercase commands and cryptic names because they want to, not because they're forced to anymore.

4. *Save trees.* Unix users generally frown on using paper listings. There are good reasons for keeping all text online and using powerful tools to manipulate it.

5. *Silence is golden.* Unix commands are notoriously silent when it comes to producing detailed error messages. Although more experienced Unix users consider this a desirable trait, many users of other operating systems would beg to differ.

6. *Think parallel.* Most tasks can be broken down into a series of smaller subtasks. These subtasks can then be run in parallel to accomplish more in the same amount of time as one large task. A significant amount of activity occurs around symmetric multiproc-

---

2.   Given words such as "dogmatic," "tenets," and "belief system," might one wonder whether the Unix philosophy describes a cultural phenomenon in addition to a technological one.

essing (SMP) designs today, an example of a general trend in the computer industry towards parallelization.

7.   *The sum of the parts is greater than the whole.* This tenet stems from the idea that a large application built from a collection of smaller programs is more flexible, and hence, more useful than a single large program. The same functional capability may exist in both solutions, but the collection-of-small-programs approach is the more forward-looking of the two.

8.   *Look for the 90-percent solution.* Doing 100 percent of anything is difficult. Doing 90 percent is far more efficient and cost effective. Unix developers often look for solutions that satisfy 90 percent of the target user base, leaving the other 10 percent to fend for itself.

9.   *Worse is better.* Unix aficionados believe that a "least common denominator" system is the one most likely to survive. That which is cheap, but effective, is far more likely to proliferate than that which is high quality and expensive. The PC-compatible world borrowed this idea from the Unix world and is making quite a go of it. The keyword here is *inclusion.* If something is accessible enough that it can include virtually anyone, it is better than something that presents itself as being "exclusive."

10. *Think hierarchically.* Unix users and developers prefer to organize things hierarchically. For example, the Unix directory structure was among the first tree-structured architectures applied to file systems. Unix has extended hierarchical thinking to other areas, such as network service naming, window management, and object-oriented development.

After reading the list of tenets, you may be wondering just what all the fuss is about. "Small is beautiful" is not such a big deal. "Doing one thing well" sounds pretty narrow-minded in and of itself. Choosing portability over efficiency isn't the sort of idea that will change the world.

Is that all there is to Unix? Is Linux just a small operating system for small minds?

Perhaps we should mention that Volkswagen built a marketing campaign around the "small is beautiful" concept that helped it sell *millions* of automobiles. Or consider that Sun Microsystems, a leading Unix systems vendor, based its strategy on putting "all the wood behind one arrowhead" or, in other words, "doing one thing well." Could all the interest in PDAs, wireless Web access, and hand-held video have something to do with *portability*?

Come. Let us begin the journey.

2

One Small Step for Humankind

About 30 years ago, when Americans drove big cars and were the envy of citizens in other countries, Volkswagen ran an ad campaign in the United States with the theme "small is beautiful." At the time, it seemed as though the German automobile manufacturer was out of touch with reality. The VW Bug, while enormously successful in Europe, looked a little silly on the American landscape, like a midget in a land of giants. Still, Volkswagen kept driving home the message that small cars were here to stay.

Then the unforeseen occurred: Middle Eastern oil ministers showed the world that, yes, indeed, they could agree on something—namely, a much higher price on a barrel of oil. By stubbornly withholding enormous quantities of crude, they tilted the supply-and-demand equation in favor of the suppliers. The price of gasoline rose well over one dollar a gallon. Gas lines appeared everywhere as the oil ministers held a knife to the world's jugular vein.

Americans, long known for their love affair with big cars, began to discover that small truly *was* beautiful. They demanded smaller cars from the auto manufacturers to salve their aching wallets, and Volkswagen was there to oblige. What was once a "funny little car" became a chic necessity.

Over time, people found that small cars enjoyed certain advantages over their larger counterparts. Besides relishing the increased gas mileage, they liked the way small cars handled—more like a British sports car than an ocean liner on wheels. Squeezing them into tight parking spots was a breeze. Their simplicity made them easy to maintain.

About the same time that Americans' affinity for small cars blossomed, a group of researchers in AT&T Bell Labs in New Jersey found that small software programs enjoyed certain advantages, too. They learned that small programs, like small cars, handled better, were more adaptable, and were easier to maintain than large programs. This brings us to the first tenet of the Unix philosophy.

2.1   Tenet 1: Small is beautiful

If you're going to write a program, start small and keep it small. Whether you're crafting a simple filter tool, a graphics package, or a gargantuan database, work to reduce it to the tiniest piece of software practicable. Resist the temptation to turn it into a monolith. Strive for simplicity.

Traditional programmers often harbor a secret desire to write the Great American Program. When they embark on a development project, it seems as though they want to spend weeks, months, or even years trying to solve all of the world's problems with one program. Not only is this costly from a business standpoint, it ignores reality. In the real world, few problems exist that cannot be surmounted using small solutions. We choose to implement such massive solutions because we don't fully understand the problem.

The science fiction writer Theodore Sturgeon once wrote "90 percent of science fiction is crud. But then 90 percent of everything is crud." The same applies to most traditional software. A large portion of the code in any program is devoted to something other than actually performing its stated task.

Skeptical? Let's look at an example. Suppose you wanted to write a program to copy file A to file B. These are some steps that a typical file copy program might perform:

1.   Query the user for the name of the source file.

2.   Check whether the source file exists.

3.   If the source file doesn't exist, notify the user.

4.   Query the user for the name of the destination file.

5.   Check whether the destination file exists.

6.   If the destination file exists, ask the user if he wants to replace it.

7.   Open the source file.

8.   Inform the user if the source file is empty. If necessary, exit.

9.   Open the destination file.

10. Copy the data from the source file to the destination file.

11. Close the source file.

12. Close the destination file.

Note that in step 10 the file is copied. The other steps perform functions that, although necessary, have little to do with copying the file. Under closer scrutiny, you'll find that the other steps can generally be applied to many other tasks besides file copying. They happen to be used here, but they're not really part of the task.

A good Unix program should provide capabilities similar to step 10 and little else. Carrying this notion further, a program strictly following the Unix philosophy would expect to have been given valid source and destination file names at invocation. It would be solely responsible for copying the data. Obviously, if all the program had to do were copy the data, it would be a very small program indeed.

This still leaves us with the question of where the valid source and destination file names come from. The answer is simple: from other small programs. These other programs perform the functions of obtaining a file name, checking whether the file exists, and determining whether it contains more than zero bytes of data.

"Now wait a minute," you may be thinking. Are we saying that Unix contains programs that only check whether a file exists? In a word, yes. The standard Unix distribution comes with hundreds of small commands and utility programs that by themselves do little. Some, such as the *test* command, perform apparently mundane functions like determining a file's readability or equivalent. If that doesn't sound very important, realize that the *test* command is one of the most heavily used Unix commands.[1]

By themselves, small programs don't do very much. They often perform one or two functions and little else. Combine them, however, and you begin to experience real power. The whole becomes greater than the sum of the parts. Large, complex tasks can be handled with ease. You can write new applications by simply entering them on the command line.

2.2   Software engineering made easy

It has often been said that Unix offers the world's richest environment for programmers. One reason is that tasks that can be difficult, if not impossible, to accomplish on other operating systems are comparatively easy to accomplish under Unix. Could it be that small programs make such tasks easy? Absolutely.

2.2.1   Small programs are easy to understand

The "all-business" approach of small programs keeps fluff to a minimum, focusing instead on performing one function well. They contain only a few algorithms, most of which relate directly to the job involved.

---

1.   Some Unix/Linux shells (command interpreters), such as *bash*, have made the test command part of the shell itself, eliminating the need to invoke a new process to run the command, thereby reducing overhead. The downside to this is that if you keep adding commands to the shell itself, eventually the shell grows to the point where nonshell commands become costly to execute because of the way Unix/Linux creates new processes. It may be better to rely on the fact that frequently used commands are typically already sitting in the kernel's buffer cache, so obtaining them from the disk, which would be prohibitively expensive timewise, would not be necessary.

Large programs, on the other hand, lean toward complexity and present barriers to understanding. The bigger a program becomes, the more it gets away from its author. The sheer number of code lines becomes overwhelming. For example, the programmer may forget which files the program's subroutines are found in or have trouble cross-referencing variables and remembering their usage. Debugging the code becomes a nightmarish task.

Some programs can be difficult to understand, whatever their size, simply because the nature of the function they perform is inherently obscure. Such programs are rare, however. Even programmers with moderate experience readily understand most small programs. This is a distinct advantage small programs have over their larger counterparts.

At this juncture, you may be wondering at what point a small program becomes a large program. The answer is, it depends. Large programs in one environment may be considered average for another. What is spaghetti code to one programmer may be daily pasta to the next. Here are some signs that suggest that your software may be departing from the Unix approach:

- The number of parameters passed to a function call causes the line length on the screen to be exceeded.

- The subroutine code exceeds the length of the screen or a standard piece of 8½-by-11 inch paper. Note that smaller fonts and taller windows on a large workstation monitor allow you to comfortably stretch the limit a bit. Just don't get carried away.

- You can no longer remember what a subroutine does without having to read the comments in the code.

- The names of the source files scroll off the screen when you obtain a directory listing.

- You discover that one file has become too unwieldy for defining the program's global variables.

- You're still developing the program, and you cannot remember what condition causes a given error message.

- You find yourself having to print the source code on paper to help you organize it better.

These warning signs are likely to ruffle the feathers of some programmers, namely those in the "big is better" camp. Not every program can be made small, they say. This world is a pretty big place, and there are some pretty big problems out there that we're trying to solve with some pretty big computers. These problems require that we write some pretty big programs.

That's a pretty big misconception.

There exists a kind of software engineer who takes pride in writing large programs that are impossible for anyone but himself to comprehend. He considers such work "job security." You might say that the only thing bigger than his ego is his last application program. Such software engineers are far too common in traditional software engineering environments.

The problem with this approach to job security is that the companies they work for inevitably realize that these engineers will eventually move on, leaving their companies holding the bag. The wiser companies take steps to prevent that. They hire individuals who understand that easily maintained software is more valuable.

No longer can the software designer say, "Heaven help the next guy." Good designers must go out of their way to make their software easy to maintain. They comment their code thoroughly—but not too thoroughly. They keep subroutines short. They pare the code down to what is absolutely necessary. This usually results in small programs that are easier to maintain.

2.2.2   Small programs are easy to maintain

Since a small program is usually easy to understand, it is likely to be easy to maintain as well, for understanding a program is the first step in maintaining it. No doubt you've heard this before, but many programmers ignore the subject of maintenance. They figure that if they took the time to write a program, then someone else will be just as willing to take the time to maintain it after them.

Most software engineers are not satisfied with maintaining other peoples' programs for a living. They believe—perhaps rightfully so—that the real money is made in writing new programs, not fixing past mistakes. Unfortunately, users don't see it quite the same way. They expect software to work the first time. If it doesn't, they get very upset with the program's vendor. Companies that fail to maintain their software do not remain in business for long.

Since maintaining software is not very glamorous work, programmers seek out ways to make the task easier or even avoid it altogether. Most cannot eliminate this duty entirely, however. If they're lucky, they probably could turn over maintenance chores to a junior individual. But more often than not, software support responsibilities usually fall upon the original author, who must settle for making the task more palatable any way he or she can. Small programs meet this need quite nicely.

2.2.3 Small programs consume fewer system resources

Because their executable images occupy very little memory, the operating system finds it much easier to allocate space for them. This greatly reduces the need for swapping and paging, often resulting in significant performance gains. A popular term in the Unix world is "lightweight" (i.e., small programs are often considered lightweight processes).

Large programs, with their huge binary images, extract a heavy price from the operating system when loaded. Paging and swapping commonly occur, causing performance to suffer. Operating system designers, aware of the resource requirements of large programs, attempt to deal with this issue by building enhancements such as dynamic loading and sharable runtime libraries. These address the symptom, not the problem.

A computer hardware engineer I met in the early days of my career often joked, "All programmers ever want is more core! All we need to stop your whining is to give you another memory board." He was partly right, of course. Give a programmer more memory, and the programs will run faster and take less time to write, greatly increasing productivity.

Reflect upon the "more core" cure for a moment. My hardware engineer friend unwittingly based his statements on the tendency of the programmers in his sphere to write large, complex programs. It's not surprising. The operating system we were using for applications development then was not Unix.

Had we been using Unix and embracing its small-program philosophy, the need for more memory would have been less evident. The joke would have been, "All programmers ever want is more MIPS!" (MIPS stands for millions of instructions per second, a popular though not necessarily accurate measure of CPU performance.)

Why has the metric of MIPS become such a hot issue in the computer world today? Because as Unix usage has become more prevalent, the use of small programs has proliferated as well. Small programs, although they usurp little system memory when executing, derive the most benefit from the injection of additional CPU horsepower. Load them into memory, and they do their job quickly, freeing up the memory for use by other small programs.

Obviously, if the CPU capacity is lacking, then each program must spend a longer time in memory before the next small program can be loaded to do its job.

Systems employing small programs benefit from additional memory, too. Larger amounts of memory allow more small programs to remain in the kernel buffer cache longer, reducing reliance on secondary storage. Smaller programs can also be laid out in the buffer cache more easily. As we shall see later, the more small programs you can run at once, the higher the overall system performance. This forms the basis of a tenet of the Unix philosophy that we'll be discussing later.

2.2.4   Small programs can easily be combined with other tools

Anyone who has ever worked with large, complex programs knows this. Monolithic programs are worlds unto themselves. In trying to provide every feature that anyone could possibly want in a single program, they build barriers that hinder easy interfacing with other applications.

What about a large application that offers many conversions to other data formats? Isn't it really more valuable than a small program that allows only one data format? On the surface, that sounds like a plausible assumption. As long as the format needed happens to be one that the application already supports, you'll get along just fine. What happens when the application must interface with a data format that it wasn't equipped to handle?

Software developers generally write large programs under the mistaken notion that they have dealt with all contingencies (i.e., their program can interface with whatever data formats exist today). This can be a problem. Although the developers can deal with today's data formats, they have no idea what new formats may come along that would render their applications obsolete. Writers of large, complex programs operate under the egotistical assumption that the future is not only predictable, it's not going to differ much from today.

Authors of small programs, on the other hand, implicitly avoid foretelling the future. The only assumption they make about tomorrow is that it will be different from today. New interfaces appear. Data formats evolve. Styles of interaction rise or fall from public favor. New hardware renders old algorithms obsolete. Change is inevitable.

In summary, you enjoy distinct advantages by writing small programs instead of large ones. Their simplicity makes them easier to write, understand, and maintain. In addition, both people and machines find them more accommodating. Most importantly, you will equip your programs to deal with situations you couldn't possibly have anticipated when you wrote them.

Look to the future. It will be here sooner than you think.

2.3   Looking at a bug

Let's take a moment to talk about a bug—not a software bug, but the other kind of bug.

A peculiar species of flying insect inhabits the area around Lake Victoria, a source of the Nile river. Spectacular video footage by the late explorer Jacques Cousteau shows this insect, known as a lake fly, congregating in thick, fog-like masses on the lake and in a nearby jungle. Similar to mosquitoes in size and appearance, they sometimes form such dense clouds over the lake that one could easily mistake them for waterspouts or small tornadoes.

Large flocks of birds often swoop down into these "bug-spouts" to feast on nature's abundance, consuming millions of insects in a single air raid. Despite the predatory onslaught, though, millions more insects persist, their shadowy swarms exhibiting few signs of attrition.

When Cousteau most closely examined the life cycle of these unusual insects, he discovered that the adults live for an exceedingly short period— about 6 to 12 hours. Even if they don't wind up as lunch for one of our feathered friends, their adult existence consists of little more than a brief flutter in the sunlight.

Just what does an insect that spends its entire adult life stage in a single day do with all that time? It attempts to propagate the species. It tries to squeeze what we human beings spend years doing into a few hours. Evidently it succeeds, for the species continues and in respectable numbers. If survival of the species is their goal, then these tiny winged nothings have set their priorities straight.

These flies have but one thing to do in life, and they do it well. Unix developers believe that software should do the same.

2.4   Tenet 2: Make each program do one thing well

The best program, like Cousteau's lake fly, performs but one task in its life and does it well. The program is loaded into memory, accomplishes its function, and then gets out of the way to allow the next single-minded program to begin. This sounds simple, yet it may surprise you how many software developers have difficulty sticking to this singular goal.

Software engineers often fall prey to "creeping featurism," as it's called in the industry. A programmer may write a simple application, only to find his creative urges taking over, causing him to add a feature here or an option there. Soon he has a veritable hodgepodge of capabilities, many of which add little value beyond the original intent of the program. Some of these inventions may have merit. (We're not talking about stifling creativity here!) But the writer must consider whether they belong in this chunk of code. The following group of questions would be a good starting point for deciding.

■ Does the program require user interaction? Could the user supply the necessary parameters in a file or on the command line?

■ Does the program require input data to be formatted in a special way? Are there other programs on the system that could do the formatting?

■ Does the program require the output data to be formatted in a special way? Is plain ASCII text sufficient?

■ Does another program exist that performs a similar function without your having to write a new program?

The answer to the first three questions is usually no. Applications that truly demand direct user interaction are rare. Most programs get along fine without having to incorporate dialogue parsers into their routines. Similarly, most programs can satisfy most needs by using standard input and output data formats. For those cases where a special format is desired, a different general-purpose program can be used to make the conversion. Otherwise, each new program must reinvent the wheel, so to speak.

The Unix *ls* command is an excellent example of a Unix application gone astray. At last count, it had more than twenty options, with no end in sight. It seems as if the number of options grows with each new version of Unix. Rather than pick on an esoteric feature, however, let's look at one of its more basic functions, specifically, the way it formats its output. *ls* in its purest form should list the names of the files in a directory (in no particular order) like this:

/home/gancarz -> ls
Txt
Doc
Scripts
Bin
Calendar
X11
Database
People
Mail
Slides
Projects
Personal
Bitmaps
Src
Memos

However, most versions of *ls* format output like this:

mail	calendar	people	slides
X11	database	personal	src
bin	doc	projects	txt
bitmaps	memos	scripts	

Listing the files in neat columns seems like a sensible thing to do, at first. But now *ls* contains code that does column formatting, a task that has little to do with listing the contents of a directory. Column formatting can be simple or complex, depending on the environment in which it is used. For example, *ls* assumes that the user is using an old-style character terminal 80 characters wide. What happens to the columns when invoking *ls* on, say, a window system in which the terminal window is 132 characters wide? Suppose the user would prefer to view the output in two columns instead of four? What if the terminal uses a variable-width character set? Suppose the user would prefer to follow every fifth line of file names with a solid line? The list goes on.

In all fairness, *ls* retains the ability to list the contents of a directory one file per line. That is about all it should do, leaving the column work to other commands better suited to formatting tasks. *ls* would then be a much smaller command (i.e., easier to understand, easier to maintain, using fewer system resources, and so on).

Since writing an application that does one thing well results in a smaller program, these two tenets complement each other. Small programs tend to be unifunctional. Unifunctional programs tend to be small.

A hidden benefit of this approach is that you remain focused on the current task, distilling it to the essence of what you're trying to accomplish. If you cannot make the program do one thing well, then you probably don't comprehend the problem you're trying to solve. In a later chapter, we'll discuss how to acquire that understanding the Unix way. For now, think small. Do one thing well.

If a lake fly on the Nile can do it, how hard can it be?

3

Rapid Prototyping for Fun and Profit

The Ramans do everything in threes.
Arthur C. Clarke, *Rendezvous with Rama*

3.1   Knowledge and the learning curve

If you take a random walk down Wall Street, you'll soon discover that the average amateur investor doesn't know what he's doing. To make money in the stock market, everyone knows you must buy low and sell high. Yet year after year, the wolves fleece the lambs out of millions of dollars. It's well documented that the little guys—meaning you and I—are usually wrong at critical turning points in the market.

Many institutional investors don't do much better either. Most pension fund managers, mutual fund portfolio managers, and professional money managers have displayed an uncanny inability to beat the market consistently year after year, though many command annual salaries over a million dollars.

Studies have shown that index funds, which invest in securities represented by an index such as the Standard & Poor's 500, have outperformed 77 percent of all mutual funds on a long-term basis. Despite the hype in the financial world about hot investment opportunities, the published records elucidate a stark reality: Most of us can do about as well as any other investor, amateur or professional, by throwing darts at the stock pages of the newspaper and buying the stocks found thereunder.

Although it is extremely difficult to beat the market consistently, some do. Peter Lynch, renowned former manager of the Fidelity Magellan Fund, racked up an impressive record in the 1980s, making his clients very wealthy. Warren Buffett, the "Oracle of Omaha," has reaped enormous profits for stockholders in Berkshire Hathaway. Sir John Templeton has made similar fortunes by seeking investment bargains the world over.

Despite their successes, these legendary investors readily admit that they don't always get it right. They tell stories of the companies in which they had complete confidence whose stocks lost over half of their value in the year they purchased them. They lament the "ones that got away," the unlikely stocks that went on to score in the 1,000 percent range and higher. Although their performance far exceeds the norm in investing, they know that they still have a lot to learn.

Other professionals have a lot to learn, too. Doctors must constantly strive to remain abreast of recent medical research developments. Accountants must learn new changes in the tax laws. Lawyers must study recent court decisions. Actuaries, salespeople, truck drivers, assemblers, plumbers, fashion designers, judges, researchers, construction workers, and engineers all have something to learn.

3.1.1   The fact is, everyone is on a learning curve

Think about it. When was the last time you met someone who knew the exact result of an action every time without fail? I'm not saying that such people don't exist. I'm only suggesting that they are rare. Such ability usually requires plenty of hard work and study, plus a dose of good luck.

Engineers offer perhaps the best living proof that most people are still learning. For example, if aeronautical engineers know everything there is to know about aeronautics, then why do they need test pilots? Why do General Motors' engineers road-test their cars? Why do computer engineers subject their products to a field test before putting them into mass production? If engineers had complete knowledge of what they were doing, quality assurance departments would be unnecessary because the quality would be built into the products during the developmental phase.

Unix engineers would write all of their programs using the *cat*[1] command.

Software engineers are particularly burdened with a steep learning curve. Software is difficult to write correctly the first time. The software engineering profession consists of constant revision, a job where trial and error are the norm, and applications are born out of countless hours of frustrating rework.

Note that we're not saying that people can never master anything. It's just that it takes longer than most people suspect. The average learning curve extends further and inclines more steeply than it first appears. So many variables exist in the world today that mastery can consume a lifetime, and complete knowledge may not even be attainable at all.

3.1.2   Even the masters know that changes are inevitable

It's a rare project indeed that doesn't require changes to the original specifications. Marketing requirements shift. Suppliers fail to deliver. Critical components may perform differently than specified. Prototypes and test runs expose design flaws. These factors make producing sophisticated technology the most delicate of tasks.

---

1.   One of the simplest of all Unix commands, *cat* directs everything that a user types into a file. Unlike a text editor or word processor, however, the *cat* command doesn't allow one to modify the text on previous lines.

Faulty communication frequently bears the responsibility for the necessity of changes. When a product's prospective end user tries to explain his needs, many gaps exist in the description. He may omit something or perhaps fail to convey with sufficient accuracy the details of what he has in mind. So the engineer uses his imagination to fill the gaps. He takes the description, looks it over, and begins to apply his own biases to the design. Sometimes the engineer tries to second-guess the end user or assumes "he really wants it this way, not that." Even worse, the engineer is often separated from the end user by corporate individuals, such as product managers, the sales team, and support personnel, who add further distortion to the end user's desired outcome.

We see through a glass darkly. Beyond the smoke and mirrors, experience dictates that we will not get it right the first time. It's better to face this axiom up front. Building into the design the assumption that changes will be needed later can reduce the cost of undertaking major revisions later when the goal is better understood.

3.1.3   Why do you think they call it software?

Software engineering requires more rework than any other engineering discipline, because software deals with abstract ideas. If people have difficulty describing hardware accurately enough to get it right the first time, imagine how difficult it is to describe something that exists only in peoples' minds and in electrical patterns traversing a microchip. The admonition, "Abandon all hope, all ye who enter here" comes to mind.

If end users could specify precisely what they wanted—if software engineers had complete knowledge of users' needs today and in the future—then we would not need software. Every program written would be placed in read-only memory (ROM) the first time around. Unfortunately, such a perfect world doesn't exist.

In my early days as a software designer, I used to strive for software perfection. I would write and rewrite subroutines until they were as fast and clean as they could be. I reviewed code repeatedly, hoping to make it even marginally better. I added new features (creeping featurism, really) as the ideas for them came along. I blissfully carried out this exercise until my boss snapped me back to reality.

"It's time to ship it," he declared.

"But it's not done yet! Just give me a couple more days to …"

"Software is never finished. It is only released."

Once a piece of software is released, no one really knows what will happen to it. Experienced engineers may have a vague notion of the consumer's demographics, the kind of environment it will be used in, and so on. But they would be hard pressed to predict reliably the eventual success or failure of any software product.

At one point, I worked as a telephone support engineer for a large computer corporation. After having worked for many years engineering the operating system, I found myself on the other side of the fence, answering questions on the programs we had written. This experience was a real eye-opener. When you're working in engineering, it's easy to fall prey to the notion that you have everything under control, that, by golly, you know how people are going to use your software.

Wrong. You may think you know what your users are going to do with your software. But what engineer, safe in his Dilbert cubicle, surrounded by engineers with advanced degrees, could have realized that:

- One Wall Street firm would lose more than $1 million an hour because of a kernel bug that kept crashing the system during the trading day. The firm was so upset that it installed a competitor's system a week later. A month later, they reinstalled the original system because, despite its flaws, it was the more reliable of the two.

- An oil company would use a system to do seismic sweeps in the Gulf of Mexico to search for oil deposits. They would acquire gigabytes of data per day, necessitating the use of more than ninety large hard drives on a system cluster. All of the data had to be available at all times. For security reasons, no one geologist could hold the key to access all of the data for fear that the individual would run off with the multibillion dollar knowledge of where next to drill for oil.

- A telecommunications company that was stashing over 10 million records per day in a database was designing a new system that would allow them to insert over 100 million records per day. Handling over 1,000 database insertions per second was difficult enough. Now they had to handle peak periods of as many as 5,000 insertions per second.

- An electric utility had one system that was the central controller for the electric power grid of one of the largest states in the United States. An outage would leave millions of people without power until the system was fixed.

The Unix developers certainly didn't know what would happen to Unix. Nor did the developers of MS-DOS, OpenVMS, and every other operating system for that matter. Every new OS—and Linux is no exception—takes its designers into uncharted waters. Their only hope consists of continually gathering progress reports and then correcting the course accordingly.

For example, did Ken Thompson realize the importance of portability when he wrote the first Unix kernel? Evidently not, for he wrote early Unix kernels in assembly language. He rewrote them later in a higher-level language, altering his original direction. Did Dennis Ritchie anticipate that C would become a universal programming language, loved and abhorred by millions of programmers? Hardly. The reissue of his classic *The C Programming Language* contained modifications to the language specification that affirmed that he didn't get it right the first time either.

So most of us are still learning. Even if we're egotistical enough to think that we know it all, someone will change the requirements on us. How then are we to build software? The next tenet holds the key.

3.2   Tenet 3: Build a prototype as soon as possible

When we say "as soon as possible," we mean *as soon as possible*. Post haste. Spend a small amount of time planning the application, and then get to it. Write code as if your life depended on it. Strike while the computer is warm. You haven't a nanosecond to waste!

The idea runs counter to what many would consider "proper engineering methodology." Most have been told that you should fully design an application before embarking on the coding phase. "You must write a functional specification," they say. "Hold regular reviews to ensure that you're on track. Write a design specification to clarify your thoughts on the details. Ninety percent of the design should be done before you ever fire up the compiler."

These guidelines sound fine in principle, but they fail to place enough emphasis on the prototype. It is in the building of the prototype that the idea is first tested for merit in a visual, realistic way. Before then, you have little more than a collection of thoughts about the way something ought to work. The concept is barely understood at that point, and it is highly unlikely that everyone perceives it in the same way. You need a consensus of perception before the project can proceed. The prototype moves toward that consensus by providing a concrete representation of the goal.

3.2.1   Prototyping is a learning process

The sooner it begins, the closer you will be to the released product. The prototype shows you what works and, most important, what doesn't. You need this affirmation or denial of the path you've chosen. It is far better to discover a faulty assumption early and suffer only a minor setback than to spend months in development meetings unaware of the Mother of All Design Flaws waiting to ambush you three weeks before the deadline.

3.2.2   Early prototyping reduces risk

Suppose you have something concrete that you can point to, and say "It's going to look like this." If you can show it to trusted users to get their reactions, you may learn that your design was on target. More often than not, your prototype will come back shot full of holes. That's OK, though. You have gained valuable design information. It is better to weather the ripples of a small group of critics than to hear a million users screaming for a recall of your product.

For every correct design, there are hundreds of incorrect ones. By knocking out a few of the bad ones early, you begin a process of elimination that invariably brings you closer to a quality finished product. You discover algorithms that do not compute, timings that keep missing a beat, and user interfaces that cannot interface. These trials serve to winnow out the chaff, leaving you with solid grain.

Most people agree that prototyping has many advantages. Even the academics who teach more traditional software engineering methodologies readily recognize its value. However, the prototyping is a means to an end, not the end in itself. The goal of all prototyping should be to build something we call the Third System. Before we can talk about the Third System, though, we need to talk about the two systems that came before it.

3.3   The Three Systems of Man

Man has the capacity to build only three systems. No matter how hard he may try, no matter how many hours, months, or years for which he may struggle, he eventually realizes that he is incapable of anything more. He simply cannot build a fourth. To believe otherwise is self-delusion.

Why only three? That is a tough question. One could speculate on several theories drawn from scientific, philosophical, and religious viewpoints. Each could offer a plausible explanation for why this occurs. But the simplest explanation may be that the design process of man's systems, like man himself, passes through three stages of life: youth, maturity, and old age.

In the youthful stage, people are full of vigor. They are the new kids on the block; they exude vitality, crave attention, and show lots of potential. As a person passes from youth to maturity, he or she becomes more useful to the world. Careers take shape. Long-term relationships develop. Influence widens in worldly affairs. The person makes an impact—good, bad, or otherwise. By the time old age sets in, the person has lost many abilities of youth. As physical prowess declines, much of the person's worldly influence fades as well. One's career becomes a memory. Resistance to change sets in. What remains is valuable wisdom based on experience.

Man's systems pass through these same stages in their development. Each system possesses characteristics that correlate with corresponding periods in life. All systems follow a path beginning at youth, transiting through maturity, and ending in old age.

Just as some men and women never reach old age, so some systems fail to mature as well. Often, this is due to external circumstances. Development plans may change. Funding for a project may be withdrawn. A potential customer may change his mind and decide to shop somewhere else. Any number of these factors could serve to prevent the system from reaching maturity. Under normal conditions, though, man carries the systems through all three stages. For our purposes we refer to these stages as the Three Systems of Man.

Most Unix developers don't know the Three Systems of Man by name, but they readily attest to their existence. Let's take a closer look at some of their characteristics.

3.4   The First System of man

3.4.1   Man builds the First System with his back against the wall

Usually the developer is under pressure to meet a deadline or satisfy other time-critical demands. This ignites a creative spark within him. Eventually the spark becomes a small flame as he spends hours in intense deliberation, turning the idea over repeatedly in his mind. Work continues. His creative instincts begin to really take hold. The flame grows brighter.

At some point, he becomes aware of aspects of his idea that go beyond simply reaching his goal. He feels as though he has stumbled upon something far more significant. The goal fades somewhat, but not before he has convinced himself that his idea provides the solution.

3.4.2   He has no time to do it right

If he had the time to do it right, he wouldn't be under any deadline pressure. So he has to improvise. But whereas the typical improvisation is one of compromise, this effort roars ahead without compromise—in the wrong direction. At least, that is what his observers conclude. When a developer's back is against the wall without time to do it right, he tends to break all the rules. It appears to his traditional-thinking coworker that he has lost his marbles under the refrigerator.

Critics often rise against him. "He can't get away with that!" they insist. "He doesn't know what he's doing. He's going about it all wrong." His response? "Yeah, it's ugly, but it works!"

The lack of time to do it right forces him to focus on the important aspects of the task and to ignore the nonessentials. As a result, he plans to leave some details to include in later versions. Note that he may never complete any later versions. The belief that he will "fill in the blanks" in the future, however, keeps him from becoming sidetracked and also provides an excuse for any shortcomings in the first version.

3.4.3   Man builds the First System alone or, at most, with a small group of people

This is partly because many people in the mainstream have little appreciation for what he's doing. They have not seen what he has seen from his vantage point, so they have no idea why he's excited. Hence, they conclude that his work is interesting, but not interesting enough for them to get involved.

A second reason that many people avoid working on the First System is more practical: Building the First System involves significant risk. No one knows whether the First System will have the characteristics that lead to the development of the Second System. There always exists a better than 80 percent chance of failure. Being associated with a First System that failed can be "career limiting," in industry jargon. Consequently, some people would rather wait until the idea is proven. (They usually become the developers of the Second System. More about them later.)

An associated risk is the possibility that an uninformed manager may declare the First System a product and turn it over to the marketing department prematurely. This usually results in sales personnel hyping a system that isn't quite ready, and it shows. System crashes are frequent and often occur at the most embarrassing times. Users develop a strong prejudice against the system because they perceive it as being of low quality. Ultimately, system sales suffer.

When a small group builds the First System, it does so with high motivation. Things happen quickly. A kind of synergy infuses the team, resulting in a strong, cohesive unit sharing a common vision and having an intense desire to bring the system to fruition. They understand the goal and toil feverishly to reach it. Working with such a group can be at once exhilarating and exhausting, not to mention very rewarding if the system succeeds.

One thing is certain: The First System is almost never built by a large group of people. Once the team grows too big for daily personal interaction among its members, productivity wanes. Personalities clash. People carry out hidden agendas. Little fiefdoms emerge as people begin to pursue their selfish interests. These occurrences dilute the goal, making it difficult to reach.

3.4.4   The First System is a "lean, mean, computing machine"

It achieves acceptable performance at minimal cost. Its developers had to take the expedient approach in most areas, forcing them to "hard-wire" much of the application code, trading features and flexibility for simplicity and speed. Frills are saved for the next version. Anything orthogonal to the system's goal is left out. The software gets the job done—and little else.

People generally marvel at the First System's performance when they compare it with a more mature system that they're familiar with. They wonder why their system cannot compete with the new kid on the disk block. They bemoan the fact that this little upstart outperforms their favorite on the popular benchmarks. It doesn't seem fair, and it isn't. Comparing a First System to a system in its nth release is inviting an apples-to-oranges comparison. The designers had different goals in mind.

The First System designers are highly focused on trying to solve the problem at hand, to get something going, to get *anything* going. Later designers usually spend much of their time trying to add new features to meet perceived market goals. When these features are taken as a whole, they often have a negative impact on performance. Yes, the later system can do more, but the new features come at a price.

3.4.5   The First System displays a concept that ignites others' imaginations

The First System causes people to engage in wild flights of fancy of the "what if…?" variety. It whets their appetite for more: more features, more functionality, more everything. People say things like, "Think of the possibilities!" and "Imagine what we could do with this at Gamma BioTech!"

The following list names some conceptual fields and technologies in which innovation is setting peoples' imaginations on fire, spawning many First Systems today:

- Artificial intelligence
- Biotechnology
- Digital imaging
- Digital music
- Electronic monetary systems and a cashless society
- Genetic engineering and cloning
- The Internet and the World Wide Web
- Interactive television
- The Mars landing
- Miniature machines
- Nanotechnology
- Quality (Six Sigma, Total Quality Management, etc.)
- Virtual reality
- Wireless technology

The concept that ignites other peoples' imaginations becomes the chief reason the Second System follows the first. If there is nothing exciting going on with the First System, then everyone concludes that it meets one's needs and (yawn!) one has something better to do. Many a First System has died in its infancy because it has failed to inspire its observers to do great and wonderful things with it.

A popular Internet repository for new First Systems is SourceForge (http://www.sourceforge.net). Some of the software presented there triggers lots of activity when people get excited about a new concept or technology. Sadly, though, not everything contributed there meets the criteria for a successful First System. Some of it simply doesn't inspire anyone. And so SourceForge has become a First System graveyard of sorts.

3.5   The Second System of man

The Second System is a strange beast. Of the three systems that man builds, it garners the most attention, often going on to become a commercial success. It does present some level of comfort and ease of entry for risk-averse individuals. Depending on the size of its market, it may capture the hearts and minds of thousands or even millions of users. Yet, ironically, in many ways the Second System is the worst of the three.

3.5.1   "Experts" build the Second System using ideas proven by the First System

Attracted by the First System's early success, they climb aboard for the ride, hoping to reap rewards by having their names attached to the system. Everyone wants to be associated with a winner.

This group of self-proclaimed experts often contains many critics of the First System. These individuals, feeling angry with themselves for not having designed the First System, lash out at its originators, spewing forth claims that they could have done it better. Sometimes they are right. They could have done a better job on certain aspects of the design. Their specialized knowledge can prove very helpful in redesigning several more primitive algorithms found in the First System. Remember: The First System's designer(s) had little time to do it right. Many of these experts know what is right and have the time and resources to carry it out.

On the other hand, some of these experts are trying to dump a load of sour grapes on someone's hard-won success. Usually this smacks of NIH, the ever-popular not invented here syndrome. Although many of these individuals could produce the First System, they were beaten to the punch. Rather than join the fun, they hope to receive credit for "having improved the obviously amateurish attempts of the original designers" by seeking to replace the First System's mechanisms with their own.

Such attitudes often invoke the ire of the First System's designers. Occasionally they fight back. Bob Scheifler, a pioneer of the popular X Window System, once responded to critics of his early design efforts in handy fashion:

"If you don't like it, you're free to write your own industry-standard window system."

3.5.2 The Second System is designed by a committee

Whereas the First System is typically the brainchild of fewer than seven people, dozens, hundreds, or, as in the case of Linux, thousands contribute to the Second System's design. The First System's success acts like a magnet. It draws in many people who may have only a remote interest in its thought-provoking ideas. Some of these people have a sincere desire to go further with the earlier designer's ideas; others just want to go along for the ride.

The Second System's design committee carries out its business very publicly. It posts meeting announcements in highly visible network repositories, user-group newsletters, and other well-known information channels. It publishes design documents that proudly display the names of all contributors. The committee tries to ensure that all participants get the credit they are due—and occasionally even that they are not due. If a committee builds a sidewalk, its members all want to write their initials in the cement.

In spite of (as opposed to because of) the activities that occur, some real design work takes place. A few committee members sign up to produce key design pieces and actually deliver quality software. Some act as "gatekeepers" for certain critical areas of the software to ensure that modifications are not only well intended, but well designed, too. Others play "devil's advocate" in helping the committee render an honest solution. Still others offer to launch points for interesting discussions that ultimately serve to clarify the new design.

Unfortunately, the design-by-committee approach involves drawbacks. It is nearly impossible for a group (an organizational body comprising at least two individuals) to agree on all salient points. For participants to feel valued, each must believe he has contributed something to the general design, no matter whether he has any expertise in the design area. It doesn't matter whether such individuals are right or wrong. They argue for the sake of their own justification, for the chance to say to themselves, "I can hold my own with these experts and, therefore, that makes me an expert, too." When you add up all the design contributors, though, you wind up with an elephant when you really wanted a gazelle.

3.5.3   The Second System is fat and slow

It possesses the opposite characteristics of the First System (i.e., where the First System was lean and mean, the Second System lumbers along like an enormous giant). If the First System required a minimum of one megabyte of memory, then the Second System refuses to run in anything less than four. People praised the First System for its high throughput on a one megahertz machine; users bemoan the Second System's turtle-like performance on a one gigahertz machine.

"It's because the Second System has more features," says the committee. "You get what you pay for."

The Second System *does* have more features. Its impressive array of capabilities accounts for part of its success, but the average user takes advantage of only a fraction of these. The rest just get in the way. As a result, the Second System runs slower because it must deal with its copious "advantages."

Often the only way to make it run faster is to buy more hardware. I've long held a belief that computer manufacturers love the Second System for this reason. In these days of portable software, most Second Systems will run on nearly any vendor's platform, provided it is big enough. To take advantage of the new technology, however, customers often must invest in new equipment. The massive size of the Second System virtually guarantees huge numbers of product sales: faster CPUs, larger disks, higher-capacity tape drives, and plenty of memory chips. This spells big profits for hardware vendors.

So the Second System is a mixed blessing. You get lots of features, some of which you might even use. And you get the chance to convince your boss that it's time to buy a new machine.

3.5.4   The world hails the Second System as a great achievement, with much pomp and circumstance

It makes a big splash in the marketplace. It garners widespread commercial acclaim for its flexibility, broad range of options, and expandability. Vendors praise its virtues: It delivers tomorrow's technology today. It goes far beyond existing systems in every respect. It's the last system you'll ever need.

The herd, overwhelmed by this hype, looks to the experts for answers. The experts willingly accommodate them. Any member of the design committee (which by now has grown to several hundred members) instantly gains respect as an expert. Others climb the ladder of credibility by critiquing the work of the design committee.

Interest in the system grows. It becomes the media's darling. Magazines spring up to track its progress. Books appear to explain its mysteries. Conferences are held for the serious-minded to discuss its future. Seminars help the less enlightened to explore its past. The phenomenon builds momentum as more followers join the ranks of the informed and the initiated.

Once the herd is convinced by all the hype that the Second System is outstanding, it remains stubbornly so. For example, the X Window System incorporates many features beyond its basic windowing capabilities. Most of these are seldom used, and their presence drastically impairs general performance. Still, X survives because it is a Second System. Despite its shortcomings, it has enough momentum to overcome any other window system in the Unix marketplace. It reigns supreme. As a Second System, no other system could take its place—except the Third System.

3.6   The Third System of man

3.6.1   The Third System is built by people who have been burned by the Second System

After several months or several years, some people begin discovering that the Second System isn't all that it was cracked up to be. They have learned that it runs slowly as it devours system resources. It was designed by experts, some of whom were experts by self-proclamation only. In trying to meet everyone's needs, the Second System has met no one's needs in any complete sense.

Soon the Second System has burned many people. They have learned that the "last system you'll ever need" is merely one of many such systems. Too many user groups have been formed. People on the fringes of the activity sphere now teach the seminars. These individuals are not as sharp as the ones who'd fed the fever earlier, so the quality level goes way down. Oceans of rhetoric fill the user conferences, as peripheral individuals, having seen the experts become famous, hope to emulate their panache. They're too late.

Eventually, the whisper that the Second System is less than perfect turns into the deafening roar of disgruntled users. Everyone becomes convinced that there has to be a better way. At that point, the world is ready for the Third System. The Third System is born out of rebellion against the Second System.

3.6.2   The Third System usually involves a name change from the Second System

By the time the Third System arrives, the First System's originators have disappeared. The most innovative people in the Second System's development have moved on to more interesting projects as well. No one wants to be associated with a future trailing-edge technology.

While the transition from the First to the Second rides on soaring wings of new hope, the transition from the Second to the Third is like a ride on the Titanic: Everyone heads for the lifeboats, as it becomes evident that perforated metal doesn't float.

The X Window System again provides us with a real-world example. X10 was the first implementation that became available as a commercial product from a major vendor. Its characteristics were typical of a First System: acceptable performance, few frills, and an exciting concept. When X11 came along, it had the essential charactersitics of a Second System in every respect and developed a wide following. Eventually a Third System will replace X11. The original name of the X Window System will probably fade from memory, as the system itself will be regarded as outdated.

3.6.3   The original concept is still intact and is regarded as obvious

Recall that the First System displayed a concept that set peoples' imaginations on fire. By the time the Third System appears, the concept will be understood and accepted by all. Everyone who uses the system acknowledges that this is the way it should be done. The idea responsible for the First and the Second Systems' development still exists in the Third System. It was tried in the fire and found true.

Examples abound of original concepts once regarded as innovative that are commonplace today. Consider ink. Once upon a time, people used a feather dipped in ink to write on parchment paper. Eventually, the fountain pen replaced the feather. In recent years (comparatively speaking), the ballpoint pen has become the standard writing tool in everyday use. In the future, you're likely to see new writing tools that make today's ballpoint pens seem archaic. Don't be surprised, though, to find that they still use ink. The use of a liquid medium to transfer our thoughts to paper is an original idea that has survived the development of several different containers. As long as we have paper, we will have ink.

3.6.4   The Third System combines the best characteristics of the First and Second Systems

The First System had very high performance, but lacked some necessary features. In the Second System, the pendulum swung back in the direction of more features at the expense of poor performance. In the Third System, the perfect balance is struck. Only the features truly needed remain. As a result, the system requires a modest number of resources and accomplishes much with them.

Another factor in the Third System's high performance is the contributions of experts—not the "pseudoexperts" spoken of earlier, but sincere, motivated individuals who possess real talent and make effective contributions to the system's evolution. Their efforts enhance the system in specific, meaningful ways. Their work, like the original enlightening ideas, stands the test of time.

Efforts to place the software in ROM have likely been unsuccessful in the first two systems because of the changing nature of software. One should never put "opinion" in ROM. By the time the Third System comes along, however, designers have a solid understanding of what works and what doesn't. Things have jelled to the point where putting the software into hardware then becomes a real possibility.

3.6.5   Finally, the Third System's designers are usually given the time to do it right

The size of the task is well understood and the risks are small because designers are working with a proven technology. Decision makers can create accurate budgets and schedules for the systems implementation.

3.7   Linux is both a Third System and a Second System

Linux came along soon after the turbulent period in the late 1980s when Unix went through a tumultuous Second System period. Signs of "Second System

Syndrome" abounded as major factions from the AT&T and Berkeley Unix communities bickered over which Unix implementation would dominate. Committees such as the Open Software Foundation were formed to try to convince users that it was "open interfaces," not the operating system philosophy, that truly mattered. Many implementations of both Unix flavors became fat and slow.

As the next major implementation of the Unix philosophy in a field of little-known systems that implement that philosophy, Linux exhibits many characteristics of a Third System. People who are tired of the bloat and bickering in the Unix world have found much joy in it. The best original Unix concepts continue to be developed under Linux. Many Linux developers are taking the time to implement kernel structures, interfaces, and GUIs correctly. And let's not overlook the obvious: Linux is a name change for Unix.

Linux also embodies a few Second Systems of its own. The system of thought known as "open source software," for example, is really taking off in the Linux world. After an extended period during which people will debate, hold symposiums on, and expound upon its merits ad nauseaum, it will move into the Third System stage where the source code for software will always be distributed freely as common practice.

3.8   Building the Third System

The goal then is to build the Third System, for it is that which gives everyone the biggest return for the effort expanded. Containing the ideal mix of features, resource consumption, and performance, it includes only those features that people actually use. It strikes a proper balance between disk space, memory, and CPU cycles versus the level of performance delivered. Users recommend it, and customers buy it year in and year out.

How do you build the Third System? You build the other two systems first. There is no other way. Any attempt to change the order merely guarantees that you will build more First or Second Systems than would otherwise be necessary.

There are some shortcuts, though. The secret is to progress from the First to the Third System as quickly as possible. The more time spent on building the first two systems, the longer it will take to achieve the Third System's optimum balance. If you keep the cycles involved in building the First and Second Systems short and iterative, you will arrive at the Third System faster.

Although producing the Third System is the goal of both Unix developers and those following "traditional" software engineering methodologies alike, the Unix developers take a radical approach. First, consider the way most software is written:

1.   Think about the system design.

2.   Build a prototype to test your assumptions.

3.   Write detailed functional and design specifications.

4.   Write the code.

5.   Test the software.

6.   Fix bugs and design flaws found during the field test, updating the specifications as you go.

The traditional software engineering methodology was invented by those who believe that it is possible to get it right the first time. "If you're going to build a system," they say, "you may as well build the Third System." The problem is, no one knows what the Third System is until it's been built.

The traditionalists like to see everything written down, as if having written specifications to the nth detail assures them that they have considered all design factors. The notion that "90 percent of the design should be complete before you write the first line of code" comes from the belief that excellent designs require forethought. They believe that by fully documenting the design, you guarantee that you have investigated all viable possibilities, and by having complete specifications, you keep things organized and ultimately increase your efficiency.

The traditional methodology results in very good specifications early on and poor specifications later. As the project gets underway, schedule pressures force the engineers to spend progressively more time on the software and less time on the specifications. Such a shift in priorities causes the specs to become out of sync with the actual product. Given a choice between a product with little documentation versus ample design specifications without a product, software developers always choose the former. People will not pay them for specifications without a product behind them.

Unix developers take an alternative view toward detailed functional and design specifications. Although their intent is similar to that of the traditionalists, the order of events differs:

1.   Write a short functional specification.

2.   Write the software.

3.   Use an iterative test/rewrite process until you get it right.

4.   Write detailed documentation if necessary.

A short functional specification here usually means three to four pages or fewer. The rationale behind this is that (1) no one really knows what is wanted, and (2) it's hard to write about something that doesn't exist. While a traditionalist may spend weeks or even months writing functional and design specifications, the Unix programmer jots down what is known about the goal at the start and spends the rest of the time building the system.

How does the Unix programmer know if he's proceeding in the right direction? He doesn't. Neither does the traditionalist. Eventually the design must be shown to the prospective end user. The difference is that whereas the traditionalist presents to the user a massive tome containing a boring description of what the system is going to be like, the Unix programmer shows the user a functional application.

The traditionalist wonders whether the final product will meet the user's needs. He cannot be sure that the user has communicated his requirements effectively, nor can he be certain that the implementation will match the specifications.

One the other hand, the Unix approach provides the user with a functional First System that he can see and touch. He begins to get a feel for how the final product will operate. If he likes what he sees, fine. If not, it's far easier to make major changes now instead of later.

Remember, though, that a characteristic of the First System is that it displays a concept that ignites others' imaginations. Viewing a live implementation of the First System sets off a creative spark in the user's mind. He starts to imagine what he might do with the product. This spark feeds on itself, and he begins to think of new uses, some of which may not have been thought of by the original designers.

At this point the Unix approach leapfrogs over the traditional engineering method. While the traditionalist's user wonders how the product will look, the Unix developer's user is already thinking of what to do with the working prototype.

For the Unix user, the iterative design process has begun. He and the developers are proceeding toward the Third System. Once the developers receive the initial reactions from the users, they know whether they are on the right track. Occasionally, the user may inform them that what he wanted is not what he received, resulting in a complete redesign. More often than not, the user will like part of the design and will provide useful commentary on what must be changed. Such cooperation between the developers and the end user is tantamount to producing a Third System that meets the user's needs in most respects.

The best time to write a detailed design specification is after the iterative design process is complete. Of course, by then a lengthy spec may not be necessary, since it is mainly intended for the developers and interested third parties to read and review. The users and the developers have been reviewing the application throughout the iterative design process, so writing a detailed spec at this point may not serve any useful purpose. If one is still required for some reason, it is far easier to document an existing application.

Some people have expressed concern that the Unix approach to software development, although quite suitable for small systems, does not work for larger ones. They argue that beginning the coding phase without a thorough design is engineering suicide. They claim that lack of adequate forethought can only lead to disaster.

We're not saying that one should plunge into coding a large system without an adequate design, however. Some amount of deliberation is necessary in order to define proper goals. It's just not very useful to document every detail before proceeding because the details are likely to change. The key here is to identify how the system might be broken into smaller components. Then each component can be architected within a much smaller design domain.

Also consider that while Unix has had the benefit of very little up-front design, it has evolved into a system capable of handling tasks once relegated to larger systems. A system of its stature traditionally would have required countless tomes of functional specifications and detailed design documents. Plenty of Unix documentation exists today through the efforts of a few enterprising technical publishers, but most of it describes designs that already exist. Original specifications are practically nonexistent.

Unlike most systems planned in the traditional way, Unix evolved from a prototype. It grew out of a series of design iterations that have transformed it from a limited-use laboratory system into one called upon to tackle the most arduous tasks. It is living proof of a design philosophy that, although unorthodox to some, produces excellent results.

4

The Portability Priority

So there I was, an attendee at the 1991 USENIX Technical Conference, strolling the halls of Nashville's Opryland Hotel, reveling in the grandiose luxury of that country music citadel, picking my way through the crowds, hoping to happen upon someone famous, and basking in the satisfaction of having just signed a publishing contract.

Things had gone extremely well. My proposal for a book on the Unix philosophy was accepted without hesitation. ("So many people need to read this book.") Contract negotiations went smoothly. ("I'd like n dollars for an advance." "Okay, you've got it.") A reasonable deadline had been set. ("We'll give you an extra couple of months to make it easier on you.") You couldn't have asked for a better situation.

To tell the truth, I was scared to death. After getting over the initial enthusiasm of signing up to author a book on a topic I'd been harping on for years, I ran headlong into a reality that I was mentally unprepared for: I now had to write the darn thing.

My past writing experience consisted of pumping out features for a regional entertainment magazine. I'd learned how to string words together. I knew about topic sentences, action verbs, and the use of passive voice. I could hook a reader and keep him interested. However, writing magazine articles only made me a great sprinter. Now it was time to run the marathon.

The first thing I did was sprint to a friend for advice. An author of several books, he had run this race before. What could I do, I asked, to get a handle on this seemingly insurmountable task?

"Buy a notebook PC," he replied.

Seeing the Neanderthal look on my face, he explained that writing a book is an all-or-nothing proposition. It takes an intense, concentrated effort to put so many thoughts down on paper. You must think about the book nearly always: while brushing your teeth in the morning, while driving to and from work, between meetings, while having lunch, during your workout at the health club, while watching television with the family, and before you go to sleep at night. The notebook PC is the only text entry device at once powerful and portable enough to enable you to write a book just about anywhere.

An amazing feat of modern microtechnology, the typical notebook PC puts most capabilities of a desktop PC in a package thinner than a three-ring binder. Weighing less than five pounds, its low-profile design makes it as easy to carry around as a college textbook. They come with hard disk drives and built-in modems, making them viable workhorses for every-day computing tasks such as calculating spreadsheets, word processing, and programming.

Some years ago, Apple Computer ran a television ad showing two executives discussing the merits of various personal computers. Both men were talking about technical specifications, and one appeared to have a profound revelation: The most powerful computer is not the one with the fastest CPU, the biggest disk drives, or the most terrific software. It is the one that is used most.

Judged solely by this criterion, the notebook PC will someday rank as the most powerful computer ever built. It doesn't have the blinding speed of, say, a laboratory supercomputer. Nor does it have the storage capacity of the latest disk farm technology. Its graphics capabilities will probably always lag behind the raciest desktop screens. Hardly the epitome of performance, it has only one real advantage: portability.

This brings us to the next tenet of the Unix philosophy. You might wish to make a special note of this one. It marks the reason Unix has nullified the longevity of thousands of man-years' worth of software development effort.

4.1   Tenet 4: Choose portability over efficiency

Software development involves choices, each of which represents a compromise. Sometimes the developer must write a short, simple subroutine because he doesn't have time to include a more sophisticated one. At other times a limited amount of RAM might be a constraint. In some situations one must avoid tying up a network connection with too many small data packets, because the network protocol in use favors transfers of large data blocks. The programmer always chooses from a set of compromises in attempting to satisfy often conflicting goals.

One difficult choice the programmer faces is portability versus efficiency. It is an agonizing one, too, because favoring efficiency results in nonportable code, while selecting portability often results in software whose performance is unsatisfactory.

Efficient software doesn't waste CPU cycles. It takes full advantage of the underlying hardware, often completely disregarding portability issues. It capitalizes on such features as graphics accelerators, cache memories, and specialized floating-point instructions.

Although efficient software is attractive from a purist's standpoint, the value of running the software on many different machine architectures tips the balance in the other direction. The reason is more financial than technical: in today's computing environments, software that runs on only one architecture sharply limits its potential marketability.

Building in portability doesn't mean that you must necessarily settle for inefficient, technically arcane software. To the contrary, obtaining optimum performance from portable software requires a higher level of technical sophistication. If the sophistication isn't there, however, you have an alternative in that you can wait until the hardware becomes available.

4.1.1   Next _____'s hardware will run faster

We used to fill in the blank with "year": Next year's hardware will run faster. Because of the speed at which hardware technology races ahead, today we can sometimes say that next quarter's or even next month's hardware may run faster. The ever-shrinking product-development cycle of today's computer manufacturers allows them to produce newer models in a fraction of the time required in the past. Vendors leapfrog each other with frequent announcements of higher performance for a lower price. As a result, whatever computer you're using today will soon feel like the clunky old behemoth in the back of your college lab.

This tendency toward tighter design cycles will accelerate, too. Today's semiconductor designers use sophisticated simulators to create follow-on versions of their microchips. As these simulators—themselves powerful computers—continue to gain speed, developers can complete designs even more quickly. These newer chips then become the engines used in tomorrow's simulators. The phenomenon snowballs with each successive generation of silicon processors. The semiconductor-design world rides a dizzying, upward-bound performance spiral.

As faster machines replace slower ones, the critical issue then becomes not whether your software takes full advantage of all the features of the hardware, but whether your software will run on the newer machines. You might spend days or weeks tuning an application for better performance on today's platform, only to find that the next hardware upgrade gives you a factor-of-ten increase in speed "free." However, your software must be portable to take advantage of the next supercomputer.

In the Unix environment, this usually translates into writing much software as shell scripts. A shell script consists of multiple executable commands placed in a single file executed indirectly by the Unix command interpreter. Because of the wide array of small, single-purpose commands found in a typical Unix distribution, all but the lowest level tasks can be constructed easily from shell scripts.

A side benefit of shell scripts is that they are far more portable than programs written in the C language. This may sound heretical, but writing your programs in C should be considered only if absolutely necessary. In the Unix environment, C lacks the portability of shell scripts. C programs often depend on definitions in header files, machine architecture sizes, and a host of other nonportable characteristics of a Unix implementation. As Unix was ported from 16-bit to 32-bit and 64-bit architectures, a significant amount of software became inoperable because C is not very portable. C is little more than the assembly language of the 1980s.

What if you want your program to run on other systems besides Unix? Other language choices exist, each with their peculiar strengths and drawbacks. If your goal is strictly one of portability, then Perl and Java fill the bill quite nicely, as implementations exist for both Unix and Windows platforms. However, just because a language has been ported to another platform besides Unix doesn't mean that the other platform adheres to the Unix philosophy and the Unix way of doing things. You will find that Java developers on Windows, for example, tend to be big proponents of interactive development environments (IDEs) that hide the complexity underneath, while Unix Java developers often prefer tools and environments that let them delve behind the graphical user interface.

4.1.2   Don't spend too much time making a program run faster

If it barely runs fast enough, then accept the fact that it already meets your needs. All time spent tuning subroutines and eliminating critical bottlenecks should be done with an eye toward leveraging performance gains on future hardware platforms as well. Resist the tendency to make the software faster for its own sake. Remember that next year's machine is right around the corner.

A common mistake that many Unix programmers make is to rewrite a shell script in C to gain a marginal edge in performance. This is a waste of time better spent obtaining constructive responses from users. Sometimes a shell script may truly not run fast enough. However, if you absolutely must have high performance and believe that you need C to get it, think it over—twice.

Certain specialized applications notwithstanding, it usually doesn't pay to rewrite a script in C.

Beware of "micro-optimizations." If—and this is a very big "if"—you must optimize a C program's performance, Unix provides *prof* and other tools for identifying the subroutines used most. Tuning routines called upon hundreds or thousands of times produces the greatest improvement for the least effort.

Another way to improve a program's performance is to examine how you deal with the data. For example, I once wrote a simple shell script that could search through more than two million lines of source code scattered across several thousand files in under a second. The secret was to create an index of the data first. Each line of the index contained a unique word and a list of all the files that the word was contained in. Most programs use less than 20,000 symbols, meaning that the index would be no more than 20,000 lines long. Searching through 20,000 lines is a relatively simple task for the Unix tool *grep*. Once *grep* located the unique word entry, it would simply print out a list of the file names associated with that word. It was very fast, yet portable due to the way that the data was being viewed.

4.1.3 The most efficient way is rarely portable

Any time a program takes advantage of special hardware capabilities, it becomes at once more efficient and less portable. Special capabilities may occasionally provide great boosts, but their usage requires separate device-dependent code that must be updated when the target hardware is replaced by a faster version. Although updating hardware-specific code provides job security for many system programmers, it does little to enhance the profit margins of their employers.

At one point in my career, I worked on a design team producing an early version of the X Window System for a new hardware platform. An engineer on the project wrote several demos that bypassed the X Window System and took advantage of the advanced graphics capabilities of the hardware. Another engineer coded a similar set of demos to run under the portable interface provided by the X Window System. The first engineer's demos really sparkled because they used state-of-the-art graphics accelerators. Incredibly efficient, they flexed the hardware's muscles to their fullest. The second engineer's demos, while admittedly slower, remained staunchly portable because they ran under X.

Eventually, the state-of-the-art graphics hardware became not-so-state-of-the-art and the company built a new, faster graphics chip set incompatible with the first. Reimplementing the first engineer's demos for the new hardware required a significant effort, more than anyone had time for. So the demos disappeared into obscurity. The portable demos that ran under X, on the other hand, were ported to the new system without modification and are probably still in use as of this writing.

When you take advantage of specialized hardware capabilities for efficiency's sake, your software becomes a tool for selling the hardware, instead of software that stands on its own. This limits its efficiency as a software product and leads you to sell it for less than its intrinsic worth.

Software tightly coupled to a hardware platform holds its value only as long as that platform remains competitive. Once the platform's advantage fades, the software's worth drops off dramatically. To retain its value, it must be ported from one platform to another as newer, faster models become available. Failure to move rapidly to the next available hardware spells death. Market opportunity windows remain open for short periods before slamming shut. If the software doesn't appear within its opportunity window, it finds its market position usurped by a competitor. One could even argue that the inability to port their software to the latest platforms has killed more software companies than all other reasons combined.

One measure of an application's success is the number of systems it runs on. Obviously, a program depending largely on one vendor's hardware base will have difficulties becoming a major contender compared to another that has captured the market on multiple vendors' systems. In essence, portable software is more valuable than efficient software.

Software conceived with portability in mind reduces the transfer cost associated with moving to a new platform. Since the developer must spend less time porting, he can devote more time to developing new features that attract more users and give the product a commercial advantage. Therefore, portable software is more valuable from the day it is written. The incremental effort incurred in making it portable from the beginning pays off handsomely later as well.

4.1.4   Portable software also reduces the need for user training

Once a user has taken the time to learn an application package, he can reap the benefits of this investment on future platforms by running the same package.

Future versions of the software may change slightly, but the core idea and the user interface supporting it are likely to remain intact. The user's experience with the product increases with each new version, transforming him from an "occasional" user into a "power" user over time.

The process of transforming users into power users has been ongoing since the very earliest versions of Unix. Most of the knowledge learned in working with the earlier versions is directly applicable to Linux today. It is true that Linux adds a few wrinkles of its own, but by and large experienced Unix users are quite comfortable in a Linux environment due to the portability of the entire user environment, from the shell to the common utilities available.

4.1.5   Good programs never die—they are ported to new hardware platforms

Have you ever noticed that certain programs have been around for years in one form or another? People have always found them useful. They have true intrinsic worth. Usually someone has taken it upon himself to write or port them, for fun or profit, to the currently popular hardware platform.

Take Emacs-style text editors, for example. While in some ways they are bad examples of Unix applications, they have long been favorites with programmers in general and Unix devotees in particular. You can always find a version around not only on Unix systems but on other systems as well. Although some Emacs versions have grown into cumbersome monoliths over the years, in its simplest form Emacs still offers a respectable "modeless" vehicle for entering and manipulating text.

Another good example is the set of typical business programs such as that found in Microsoft Office and similar products. People have found that modern business environments usually require desktop programs such as word processors, spreadsheets, and presentation tools in order to function effectively.

No single individual, company, organization, or even nation can keep a good idea to itself, however. Eventually, others take notice, and "reasonable facsimiles" of the idea begin to appear. The intelligent entity, recognizing an idea's merit, should strive to implement it on as many platforms as practical to gain the largest possible market share. The most effective way to achieve this end is to write portable software.

CASE STUDY: The Atari 2600

Let's look at the Atari 2600, otherwise known as the Atari Video Computer System (VCS). The VCS was the first successful home video game system, a product in the right place at the right time. It captured the imagination of a people that had just sampled Space Invaders at local pubs and arcades and was ready to bring the new world of video games into the living room. The first cartridge-programmable game console, it launched an entire industry bent on bringing the joys of games once found only in campus labs and software professionals' hidden directories to the family television screen. If programmers have an affinity for games, it is minuscule compared to the interests of mainstream America and, for that matter, the world at large.

High on the price-performance curve when it was introduced, the 2600 gave you reasonable capabilities for your money. The 8-bit console sold for around $100 or so. It came with a couple of joysticks and a pair of potentiometers known as paddle controllers. Atari supplied it with "Combat," a cartridge programmed with a variety of two-person battle games incorporating tanks, jets, and Fokkers.

Atari made comparatively little money on sales of the console. The big profits came from the sale of the game cartridges. With prices ranging from $14 to more than $35 each, these units became the bread and butter of Atari and a slew of smaller software houses hoping to capitalize on the video game craze. From Atari's standpoint, once the software engineering investment to develop a cartridge was recovered, the rest was pure gravy.

A friend of mine found a job at a software house that produced cartridges for the 2600. He explained that it was quite a feat to squeeze, say, a chess game or a "shoot-em-up" into less than 8K of ROM. It was like jamming twenty people into a Volkswagen Bug; not everyone gets a chance to look out the windows.

In writing the code for the game cartridges, he wrote some of the most efficient—and nonportable—software in his career. He treated instructions as data and data as instructions. Certain operations were performed during horizontal retrace, the time when the light beam on a television set, having finished painting the last dot on the right side of the screen, returns to the left side. Every possible shortcut had to be taken to conserve memory. His code was at once a thing of beauty and a software maintainer's worst nightmare.

Sometime during the reign of the 2600, Atari introduced the 800, a 6502-based system that became the flagship of its home computer line. The

800 was a true computer in the sense that it had a typewriter-style keyboard and interfaces for secondary storage and communications devices. Selling for close to $1,000, the 800 posed little threat to the 2600's captive niche—until the price of memory chips dropped.

Because of competitive pressures from other vendors and the 800's popular extended graphics capabilities, Atari fell under heavy pressure to produce a video game machine for the mass market that could run the 800's software. The new machine, dubbed the 5200, made it possible for the mass-market computer illiterates to run the same games that the techies were playing on the 800.

Once the mass market had discovered this amazing new machine, it dumped the primitive looking 2600 for the smoother graphics of the 5200. The bottom then promptly fell out from under Atari 2600 game cartridge prices. Dealers, expecting the demise of the 2600, began slashing the prices on their existing inventories, virtually flooding the market with cut-rate 2600 cartridges. This drove prices down even further, taking down a few software houses in the process.

The pain didn't end there for the cartridge producers. Most popular games on the 2600 became instant hits on the 5200 as well—but not before they were completely rewritten to run on the new hardware platform. Since the code in the 2600 cartridges was so efficient, it lacked anything remotely portable. This meant the software had to be rewritten at great expense.

The point here is that although the game-cartridge software was arguably the most efficient ever written, its value plummeted the day the new hardware was announced, all because it was not portable enough to be recompiled and reused on the 5200. Had the code been portable, the video-game phenomenon would have evolved quite differently. Atari would probably have become the world's largest supplier of software.

Finally, note that you will pay as little as a few pennies on the dollar for an Atari 2600 game cartridge today, and you will do so mostly out of nostalgia. You still cannot purchase the most powerful versions of Microsoft Office for less than several hundred dollars. Part of the reason for this is that Microsoft Office migrated from one platform to the next as Intel Corporation released progressively more powerful versions of its 8086 processor. This kept Office on the leading edge of the power curve. But that position on the power curve comes at a high cost.

The developers of Office must keep a sharp eye on the future of Open-Office and other Office clones appearing in the Linux marketplace, however.

Some of these have greater inherent portability than Office. This could mean that they might be more adaptable in the future as business technology evolves. Microsoft could find itself having to dig ever deeper into its pockets to maintain Office's dominance. As long as Intel continues to produce CPU chips with instruction sets that are backward compatible, Microsoft Office (and for that matter, Microsoft Windows itself) will be relatively inexpensive to port. If someone came out with a machine so advanced that everyone wanted its capabilities even if it weren't Intel-compatible, Microsoft would face the gargantuan task of porting Windows and Office to the new architecture—or else.

The moral of the story? Portability pays. Anything else is merely efficient.

✳ ✳ ✳

Thus far we have been discussing the merits of portable software versus efficient software. Code moved easily to a new platform is far more valuable than code that takes advantage of special hardware features. We have seen that this axiom can be measured in real terms, (i.e., in dollars and cents). To preserve its profit base, a software company should strive for portability in its products, possible foregoing efficiency in the process.

Portable code, however, goes only halfway toward meeting the goal of portability. All applications consist of instructions and data. By making the instructions portable, you ensure that your code will be ready to run on next year's machine. What then happens to your data? Is it left behind? Not at all. The Unix programmer chooses to make not only the code portable, but the data as well.

How does one make one's data portable? The next tenet of the Unix philosophy is one solution.

4.2   Tenet 5: Store data in flat text files

"Flat text files" means that you store all data as text. Period. Binary format files are *verboten*. No special file-system formats are allowed. This rules out a host of interesting, but nonportable, formats invented by vendors for propriety purposes. Data files should consist of only a stream of bytes separated by line feed characters or "newlines," in the lingo of the Unix world.

Many consider this a bitter pill to swallow, but Unix programmers swear that this is the best way. Here is the secret: While data is kept on any kind of storage media, eventually it must go somewhere. Data sitting on a disk diminishes in value. For data to remain alive and valuable, it must move occasionally. Otherwise it should be archived and deleted.

Data that goes nowhere is dead data.

If you expect to move your data easily, you must make it portable. Any impediments to data movement, whether unintentional or by design, place limits on your data's potential value. The longer your data must sit somewhere, the less it will be worth when it finally arrives. The problem is, if your data is not in a format that is useful at its destination, it must be converted. That conversion process takes time. Every second spent in data conversion eats away at your data's value.

The Cable News Network (CNN), won top honors in 1991 for its coverage of the Persian Gulf War. CNN provided the world with graphic scenes of the conflict and did it quickly. Many people rushed home to their television sets every night to watch the events unfold. Would the CNN coverage have been as riveting if the production staff had spent several days converting the videotape from beta to VHS, airmailed the tapes to Atlanta, and showed them only during prime time?

So it is with your data. If it takes extra time to convert your data from a nonportable format to move it, the data will not be worth as much when it gets there. The world moves much too quickly to wait for your data.

4.2.1   Text is a common interchange format

Text is not necessarily the highest performing format; it's only the most common one. Other formats have been used in some applications, but none has found such wide acceptance as text. In nearly all cases, data encoded in text can be handled by target platforms.

By using text, you eliminate the difficulties of converting your data from one binary format to another. Few binary formats are standardized. Each vendor has defined its own binary encoding, and most of them are different. Converting from one vendor's format to another's can be an arduous task requiring anywhere from several days to several months. This time would be much better spent using the data.

4.2.2   Text is easily read and edited

It is possible to examine text data without conversion tools. If the data doesn't look right, you can use a standard text editor to modify it. Specialized tools are not required. You don't need a separate editor for each kind of data file. One size fits all.

The real power of text files becomes apparent when developing programs that use pipes under Unix. The pipe is a mechanism for passing one program's output to another program as input without using a temporary file. Many Unix programs are little more than a collection of smaller programs joined by a series of pipes. As developers prototype a program, they can easily check the data for accuracy at each point along the pipeline. If there is a problem, they can interrupt the flow through the pipeline and figure out whether the data or its manipulator is the problem. This greatly speeds up the development process, giving the Unix programmer a significant edge over programmers on other operating systems.

Text files also simplify the Unix user's interface with the system. Most administrative information under Unix is kept in flat text files and made available for universal inspection. This significantly reduces the amount of time spent by individuals in accessing the information to accomplish their daily work. Information about other users, systems on the network, and general statistics can be gleaned with minimal effort. Ironically, portable data here results in greater efficiency.

4.2.3   Textual data files simplify the use of Unix text tools

Most Unix environments contain dozens of utilities for transmitting, modifying, and filtering text. Unix users employ these utilities in many combinations to do their daily work. the following lists some of the more popular ones with a brief description of their functions:

awk	Perform functions on text arranged in fields
cut	Extract specific columns from lines of text
diff	Perform a line-by-line comparison of two text files
expand	Convert tab stops to spaces
expr	Extract part of a string from another string
fmt	A simple paragraph formatter
grep	Extract lines from a file containing a specified text string
head	Display the first n lines of a file
lex	Perform lexical analysis of a text stream
more	Display a text file one screen at a time

paste	Convert a single text column into multiple columns
roff	A comprehensive text formatter and typesetter
sed	A noninteractive text line editor
sort	Sort a column of text
tail	Display the last n lines of a file
test	Compare two strings for equality
tr	Replace selected characters in a file
wc	Count the number of lines, words, or characters in a file

Many of these utilities have other features besides those mentioned in the above list. For example, *awk* can mix alphabetical and numeric text interchangeably. *Test* can check the modes of files to learn whether they are writable by the user. *Lex* provides an interface to the C programming language driven by matching string expressions in the input stream. *Sed* by itself is powerful enough to replace commands like *grep, head,* and *tail*.

The mixed-mode capabilities of these commands tend to blur the line between text and what is traditionally thought of as data. Hence, it is easier to represent in textual form that which was formerly stored in binary files. Unix programmers usually store numerical data in text files because the Unix environment provides a rich set of tools to manipulate those files.

Storing data as text and then manipulating it with a diverse set of small, text-oriented tools makes Unix systems formidable data processors. With tools such as *awk*, *sed*, and *grep* available on virtually all Unix and Linux systems, the ability to select, modify, and move data becomes more accessible to everyone. Even people who aren't programmers find it easy to read and interpret data stored in flat text files.

The developers of Hewlett-Packard's OpenVMS[1] operating system may be right in thinking that most people are afraid of the computer. Instead of shielding users from the system, though, Unix takes them inside it. It leads them through the labyrinthine logic trails, while they hold onto their last vestige of familiarity—namely, their data in a format that can be read and

---

1.   OpenVMS was originally developed by Digital Equipment Corporation. Digital Equipment Corporation was later acquired by Compaq, which was later acquired by Hewlett-Packard.

understood. For all the criticism of the "unfriendly Unix user interface," Unix may well be the friendliest system of all. Users can always look at their data without having to be system gurus skilled at interpreting complex binary file formats.

4.2.4 Increased portability overcomes the lack of speed

Throughout this discussion, you've probably been thinking, "Yeah, portability is nice, but what about performance?" It's true that using flat text files slows things down a bit. It takes two or three characters to represent the contents of one binary byte. So you're potentially talking about a 3:1 reduction in performance. This sounds significant, but it really isn't at all, except in high-resolution real-time applications or the rare multiterabyte data warehouse application. Even in, say, a huge data warehouse application, however, the user has the ability to absorb and analyze only a minuscule (by human standards, anyway) abstraction of the data. So at some point, the amount of data is reduced to an amount that is insignificant by CPU-cycle standards.

Eventually, every application program is ported to a new system, or else it becomes extinct. The unrelenting progress of computer manufacturers assures us that what may have been prohibitively expensive today will be dirt cheap tomorrow. It doesn't pay to run an application on a slow system that is becoming increasingly costly to maintain.

The payoff in using text comes when you must port your application to a new architecture. If you had enough foresight to make your program portable, then with text it becomes a trivial matter to move your data to a new platform as well. Woe to software engineers who must port both data and program code. The data will be stale by the time it ever sees the new memory boards. The cumulative time lost by a 3:1 performance reduction pales in comparison with the weeks or months lost in moving the data to the new platform.

4.2.5 The lack of speed is overcome by next year's machine

We've acknowledged that text files impose a drag on performance. You could possibly realize up to a 3:1 reduction in speed. However, if the application meets today's minimum performance requirements, you can expect that next year's machine will yield a dramatic improvement—if your data can be ported.

As of this writing, next year's machine usually offers enough additional computing power to render any of today's performance concerns about text files superfluous. In other words, if your application barely performs adequately today, its speed will be ample tomorrow. In a few years you may even have to start thinking about how to slow it down so people can use it!

CASE STUDY: One Unix Philosopher's Bag Of Tricks

We have seen that given a choice between high efficiency and high portability, Unix programmers' preference weighs heavily with the latter. As a result, their applications are often among the first to run on new platforms as they become available. This gives their software a definite edge in the marketplace. In a world where windows of opportunity open overnight and slam shut as soon as a month later, pursuing the portability priority can mean the difference between being an industry leader or being one of the others that wish they were.

How did Unix programmers come to embrace such beliefs? Most early software engineers weren't taught the importance of portability in school, at least not with any sense of conviction. More likely, they learned the value of portable code and data the best way: through firsthand experience.

Most Unix "gurus," as they're called, carry a collection of programs and shell scripts that make up their personal tool kit. These tools have followed them as they've moved from machine to machine, job to job, and company to company. For purposes of illustration, let's look at a Unix philosopher's bag of tricks.

My personal collection of tools has varied through the years. Here is a partial sample of those that have stood the tests of time and portability:

`cal`	A shell script front end to the Unix *cal* program that allows you to specify textual names for months instead of numbers. Borrowed from *The Unix Programming Environment* by Brian Kernighan and Rob Pike.[2]
`cp`	A "fumble finger" front end to the Unix *cp* program that prevents you from unintentionally overwriting an existing file
`l`	Runs the *ls* command with the *–F* switch specified
`ll`	Runs the *ls* command with the *–l* switch specified
`mv`	Similar to the *cp* script, it prevents you from unintentionally overwriting an existing file by renaming another file to a file with the same name.
`vit`	Invokes the *vi* editor with the *–t* flag for use with tags and tag files. Tags make it easy to locate subroutines in a collection of files.

---

2.   © 1984, Bell Telephone Laboratories, Inc.

I have converted some scripts into aliases for use with the C shell, an interactive command interpreter originally found on Berkeley Unix systems. Aliases allow you to specify alternative forms of heavily used commands without having to resort to putting everything into shell scripts. Like shell scripts, they, too, are portable.

I originally built these tools under Unix Version 7 on a Digital PDP-11/70 at a small company engaged in the manufacture of newspaper composition systems. As the company added new systems for software development, I moved them to PDP-11/34, PDP-11/44, and LSI-11/23 systems also running Unix. This doesn't sound like a grand feat, given the renowned compatibility of the PDP-11 line, but wait. It gets better.

Eventually, I left the company in pursuit of other career opportunities, taking my tools with me on a nine-track tape. The C programs and shell scripts had soon found a home on a Digital VAX-11/750. The VAX-11/750 had more horsepower than the smaller PDP-11s I'd been using. Consequently, they ran a bit faster at the new company. The tools picked up even more speed when the company replaced the VAX-11/750 with a VAX-11/780. All this happened without modifications to the tools whatsoever.

About that time, workstations—those wondrous you-mean-I-can-have-the-whole-darn-computer-to-myself boxes—vaulted onto the scene. Everyone flocked to buy the hot new machines from Sun Microsystems, my employer included. So the tools that had been moved from the PDP-11 to the VAX line suddenly found themselves running without modifications on Sun workstations.

Having spent the greater part of my software engineering career in New England, I found the latest equipment from the original digital equipment maker to be fairly common within a hundred miles of Boston. Again, I ported my old reliable C programs and shell scripts to the Digital line, this time to the VAX 8600 series and later to the VAX 8800 series. Again, the tools ran without modification.

Necessity is the mother of midnight invention. A software engineer I was working with had noticed a large cache of Digital Professional 350s collecting dust in a warehouse. An enterprising individual concluded that these 350s would make fine personal computers for us at home, especially if they were running Unix. So he proceeded to port a version of Unix to the 350. My tools soon followed.

Then along came the parade of VAXstations and the early versions of the X Window System. A portable window system was a major step in the evolution of useful user interfaces. Despite all the whiz-bang effects of a window system, I still found that my favorite tools were very helpful in an *xterm* (terminal emulator) window.

But the computer business is a risky business. You must remain flexible to stay on top. To a software engineer, flexibility translates into portability. If your software does not port to the newest machine, it will die. Period. So when the RISC-based DECstation 3100s and 5000s came along, it was a port-or-die situation. My tools displayed their penchant for portability again.

Today my little bag of tricks runs on a variety of boxes, large and small, under various Linux distributions—without modification.

These C programs and shell scripts have seen more than twenty years of daily use, on different vendors' machines, under a variety of Unix versions, on everything from 16-bit to 32-bit to 64-bit CPU architectures running the gamut from PCs to microcomputers to mainframes. How many other programs do you know of that have been used for so long in so many environments?

My experience with these tools is hardly unusual. Unix and Linux programmers the world over have similar stories to tell. Nearly everyone who has used Unix or Linux on more than a casual basis has his or her own collection of goodies. Some undoubtedly have far more comprehensive tool kits than mine. Others have probably ported their software to even more platforms, all without modification and with virtually no user retraining.

The record of portability speaks for itself. By making your programs and data easy to port, you build a long-lasting, tangible value into your software. It's that simple. Code and data that opt for efficiency lock themselves into the architecture for which they were designed. With the onrush of new platforms, obsolescence preys on the nonportable. Instead of watching the worth of your software investment shrink to zero with each industry announcement, plan ahead. Design with portability in mind.

On the day you hold in your hands your first 100 PHz (petahertz) laptop with 500 exabytes of storage[3]—and this may be sooner than you think—be sure your software will be ready for it.

---

3.   One petahertz equals one quadrillion (10^{15}) hertz. An exabyte is approximately one quintillion bytes or about one billion gigabytes. And consider that next year's model will be even faster!

5

Now That's Leverage!

Be fruitful and multiply.
Genesis 1:28

If you want to make a lot of money, sell Tupperware. You know, those plastic storage containers that seal in freshness and fill your fridge with scads of hopelessly unlabeled pastel bowls. The next time you wish you had another six feet of kitchen cabinets, consider how the universal appeal of these containers has made them a household fixture. Everyone has at least one Tupperware container tucked away somewhere.

Individual dealers sell Tupperware products via the "party plan:" They stage informal gatherings at the homes of people who sponsor them in return for a nominal share of the proceeds. Sponsors stay busy at these parties, giving product demonstrations, offering hints and tips, taking orders. It's hard work. A few of them even make a little money at it.

My aunt sold almost a million dollars' worth of Tupperware products one year.

When I heard this, my first thought was, "That's a lot of bowls!" After getting used to the idea that we would soon have a new millionaire in the family, I started wondering how she had done it. She was just a regular person. You know, one of the family. Hardly the type you would expect to be well on her way to riches.

I knew she had worked very hard, continually soaring to new heights with her seemingly limitless energy. Everywhere she went, she would talk up a storm about how good Tupperware products were. Sometimes she would visit our house while on vacation and she would toil very late, catching up on her business paperwork.

Still, for all her grueling determination, it just didn't fit. The math simply did not work out. Suppose that a bowl sold for an average price of $7. To sell a million dollars worth would require selling 142,858 of them. If you assume that she worked six days a week for fifty weeks, then she would have to have sold 477 bowls a day.

Now, my aunt is a terrific salesperson. Her sales prowess is legendary. If it can be sold, she can offer it to you and you will buy it. But 477 bowls a day, every day (except Sunday), was more than I thought even she could do. After all, one has to rest occasionally. Besides she was raising a family at the time.

So one day I pulled her aside and asked her how she sold a million dollars' worth of Tupperware products in one year. Her reply? "Silly! I didn't sell all those bowls. I got someone to sell them for me!"

She explained that she started out selling Tupperware at home parties on weeknights. On a good week, she figured, she could do five parties and sell between $100 and $150 worth at each. Eventually she realized that, while she was a fine plastics peddler, there were only so many hours in the week in which to peddle. So she found twenty other people and sold them on the idea of selling Tupperware. Each of them would hold five parties weekly, making a total of one hundred a week between them. She would sell her bowls to those twenty people for a small profit from each. It wasn't long before those twenty people understood the value of "pyramiding" themselves. Soon some had twenty people selling bowls for each of them.

The rest is multilevel marketing history.

Then my aunt shared a potent bit of wisdom: No matter how bright, energetic, or aggressive you are, there is only so much of you to go around. If you want to be fantastically successful, then you must multiply your effect on the world. It's not enough to have a high IQ or the ability to sell winter parkas in Hawaii. You need to set enterprises in motion that distribute and enhance the impact of your talents and abilities. For every hour of your labor, expect a yield of five, a hundred, or even a thousand times your efforts.

The key word here is leverage. Like the lever and fulcrum you studied in high school physics class, any movement at one end of the lever is experienced at the other end. If the fulcrum is placed in the exact center of the lever, a one-to-one correspondence exists between the opposite ends of the lever. If one end moves up five units, then the other end goes down by five units. However, if you stand at one end of the lever and place the fulcrum close to you, a small movement at your end can effect a much larger motion at the opposite end. The trick, then, is to find a way to move the fulcrum closer to you in an endeavor. In other words, you want a one-inch move on your end of the lever to send the other end halfway to the moon.

One reason for the growing success of Unix is its ability to help the leveraging efforts of individuals. This didn't just happen as a matter of chance. It came about by way of cooperative design by dozens and later hundreds of programmers. They recognized that they could only do so much by themselves. But if they could multiply their effects, they could take advantage of software leverage.

5.1   Tenet 6: Use software leverage to your advantage

Let's suppose you're one of the world's best programmers. Every piece of code you write turns to gold. Your applications become instant hits the day they're released. Critics on the Web sites shower your work with praise, and your software adorns the covers of the trade rags. Your programs are truly unique.

Unfortunately, being "one of a kind" poses a problem for you. The uniqueness that distinguishes your work becomes the chain that binds you. If you do all the work yourself, you can only do so much. Unless you can find a way to off-load some of it, you will burn yourself out long before you achieve your maximum potential.

5.1.1   Good programmers write good code; great programmers borrow good code

The best way to write lots of software is to borrow it. By borrowing software, we mean incorporating other people's modules, programs, and configuration files into your applications. In producing a derivative work, you augment the previous developers' efforts, carrying their implementations to new heights of utility. Their software becomes more valuable as it finds a home in more applications; your software becomes more valuable because your investment in it has been reduced relative to its return. It's a mutually beneficial situation.

Although you may have lowered your investment in an application, you must not necessarily settle for reduced profits. Applications built by integrating other people's code can sell for considerable amounts of money. They also tend to grab significant market share because they usually reach the market before those developed by competitors. The old adage, "the early bird gets the worm," holds especially true here. If you can be the first with a hot new application, it doesn't matter that you achieved your position by using other people's work. Potential customers just want to know whether your software can do the job. They are less interested in how your software works than in what it can do for them.

Leveraging other people's code can result in powerful advantages for the individual programmer, too. Some programmers believe that they protect their job security by writing the code themselves. "Since I write good code, I'll always have a job," they reason. The problem is, writing good code takes time. If you have to write every line of code used in an application, you will appear slow and inefficient. The real job security belongs to the software developer who can cut and paste modules together quickly and efficiently. Developers like that often produce so much software in a short time that companies generally consider them indispensable.

I recall a less-than-top-notch software engineer who couldn't program his way out of a paper bag. He had a knack, however, for knitting lots of little modules together. He hardly ever wrote any of them himself, though. He would just fish around in the system's directories and source code repositories all day long, sniffing for routines he could string together to make a complete program. Heaven forbid that he should have to write any code. Oddly enough, it wasn't long before management recognized him as an outstanding software engineer, someone who could deliver projects on time and within budget. Most of his peers never realized that he had difficulty writing even a rudimentary sort routine. Nevertheless, he became enormously successful by simply using whatever resources were available to him.

5.1.2   Avoid the not invented here syndrome

Symptoms of NIH appear in the finest of organizations. When a group refuses to recognize the value of another group's application, when one would prefer to write an application from scratch instead of using one "off the shelf," when software written elsewhere isn't used simply because it was written elsewhere, NIH is at work.

Contrary to popular belief, NIH does not expand creativity. Viewing another's work and declaring that you could do it better doesn't necessarily make you more creative. If you start from scratch and redesign an existing application, you're engaging in imitation, not creativity. By avoiding NIH, however, you open doors to new and exciting worlds of engineering design. Since less time is spent rewriting existing routines, you can devote more time to developing new functional capabilities. It's like starting out in a Monopoly game owning hotels on Boardwalk and Park Place. You don't have to spend half the game trying to acquire the property and build the hotels.

NIH can be especially dangerous with today's emphasis on standardization in the software industry. Standards drive software vendors toward commoditization. All spreadsheets begin to look alike, all word processors provide the same capabilities, and so on. The resulting oversupply of available software to accomplish everyday tasks drives prices down, thus limiting profitability. Every vendor needs a spreadsheet, a word processor, and so on, just to stay in the game. But few vendors can afford to produce those staples from scratch. The most successful companies will be those that "borrow" the software, leaving them the opportunity to create enhancements or "added value," in industry jargon.

I once worked with a team of software engineers who were working on a GUI for a window system. We had an idea to mimic another popular interface on the market. Since the other was so successful, we reasoned, then ours would surely be a hit as well. The plan was to rewrite the user interface from scratch, making it more efficient in the process.

We had two obvious strikes against us. First, in attempting to write a more efficient program, we would have to take some steps that would result in nonportable software. By "hardwiring" the application to our target architecture, we severely limited the size of our potential market. Second, it would take several months to write the user interface from scratch. While we were busy writing our own user interface, the developers of the one we were imitating weren't exactly twiddling their thumbs. They were busy adding features and enhancements to their software. By the time we released our version, theirs would be at least a generation removed from ours.

Fortunately for us, we were too blind then to realize that the other company's user interface would have evolved considerably while we were developing ours. Instead we became concerned that we might become involved in a patent infringement suit if our software looked and felt too much like the one we were bent on imitating. So we ran our ideas past one of our corporate lawyers. He opened our eyes to a more interesting possibility.

"Instead of duplicating the other company's work, why not use their software in our product?" he asked. We all took a deep swallow on that one, and the letters P-R-I-D-E got stuck in our throats. His suggestion dealt a real blow to the NIH tradition we had carefully nurtured and guarded over the years. The toughest part was admitting that his idea made sense.

So we set about learning how to incorporate the other vendor's software into our product and enhance it. It was a painful endeavor, given our history of wanting to do it our own way. Eventually, we released a set of programs built using the other software as a base. The result? Customers praised our efforts at compatibility. They bought our product because it offered value above and beyond competitors' packages while remaining compatible with de facto industry standards. We had a winner on our hands.

Take note of the phrase "added value," for it holds the key to success in the software realm of the 1990s and beyond. As computer hardware has become a commodity, so software will proceed down the same path. The various ongoing standardization efforts virtually guarantee this. Prices of software will drop, since every major vendor will be providing similar capabilities. Software companies will then have two options: They can watch their profit margins shrink to zero or else preserve them by adding value to standard applications. They must invent features that differentiate their products from industry standards as they simultaneously retain compatibility with those same standards. To survive, companies must meet the challenge of the conflicting goals of uniformity and independence. The way to win will be to add glitter to the wheel, not to reinvent it.

Sounds a lot like the hurrah coming from the Open Source movement, doesn't it? You're catching on. Later we shall see how Linux vendors and consultants take the idea of added value and turn it into the basis for a viable business model.

NIH adherents are under attack on several fronts in today's business environment. New high-capacity storage technologies, such as DVDs, pose a huge threat. These same shiny disks used to distribute the latest movies can also store over 100 gb of programs and data cheaply. Inexpensive media like these have the potential to alter the software landscape permanently. As CDs and DVDs have become commonplace, storage technology has taken an irreversible leap forward.

In a recent visit to a local PC show, I discovered a CD containing over 2,400 programs selling for a mere $5. (Admittedly, this is an example of "low-tech" these days, but it further illustrates the point.) It will be difficult to justify rewriting programs available for less than a penny elsewhere—unless you're a software developer who can live for months on a few cents.

Perhaps the biggest threat to NIH comes from high-speed Internet access technologies such as cable modems and DSL. These make it possible for anyone to download thousands of programs for free. They don't even have to go to a PC show to find them. They're readily a few mouse clicks away.

When good software becomes available at zero cost, NIH all but disappears. Any method of software development that does not incorporate software developed by others becomes too expensive. This is not to say that no new code will ever be written. Most new software will either (1) enhance and extend existing software, or (2) realize a completely new application. Linux and the Open Source community are uniquely positioned to take advantage of either scenario.

5.1.3   Allow other people to use your code to leverage their own work

Software engineers tend to hoard their source code. It's as if they believe they have written a unique contrivance, a magic formula that would change the world whose secret they alone possess. They harbor subconscious fears that if they give the source away, they will no longer control this mysterious pearl of great price.

First, software is no magic formula. Anyone with a reasonably logical mind can write the stuff. You can be clever or trite, but all software boils down to a series of calculated statements that cause the hardware to perform certain well-defined operations. A programmer who has never seen the source code can disassemble even the best program. Disassembly is a slow, tedious process, but it can be done.

What about the question of control? A commonly held belief in the computer world is that whoever controls the source code "owns" the program. This is partly true. A company that holds the source code exercises some authority over who modifies a program, who can obtain runtime licenses for it, and so on. Unfortunately, this ability to control the life of a piece of software protects only the company's temporal investment in the program's development, not the software itself. It cannot prevent the onset of imitators (clones) that seek to emulate its features and functions. Most ideas that are good enough for a company to invest in are also good enough for its competitors to invest in. It's only a matter of time before imitations appear as other vendors strive to catch the wave. The most successful software then becomes the one that appears on the most computers. Companies operating in a proprietary fashion find themselves at a significant disadvantage here.

Unix owes much of its success to the fact that its developers saw no particular need to retain strong control of its source code. Most people believed it lacked any real value. They regarded Unix as a curious oddity, suitable for research labs and universities, but not much else. No one—except its developers—considered it a serious operating system. Consequently, one could obtain its source code for a pittance.

Soaring development costs caused hardware vendors to reduce their investment in the software needed to make their platforms marketable. A pittance for an operating system soon looked like a very good deal. Unix flourished as a result. Whenever anyone wanted to save the expense of developing an operating system for a new computer, they turned to Unix. Even today many still consider it among the least expensive operating systems available.

Low cost has made Linux the platform of choice for many software houses today. By building on the kernel, programming interfaces, and applications provided by the Linux system developers, these companies use software leverage to tremendous advantage. In avoiding the cost of writing an operating system and a set of suitable applications, they can focus instead on enhancing their own applications to provide superior and value-added customizations. This puts them in a stronger position in the software world than those companies that must first invest in operating system development before they can produce applications. Companies operating in this fashion often sell *expertise,* rather than the software itself. The software business then becomes one where companies provide consulting and customization services, instead of functioning as software manufacturers.

5.1.4   Automate everything

One powerful way to leverage software to your advantage is to make your machines work harder. Any process you do manually today that your computer can do is a waste of your time. Even in modern engineering labs, surprisingly many skilled personnel still rely on crude, manual methods to accomplish their daily tasks. They ought to know better, but old habits die hard. Here are some clues that you may be working harder than necessary, while your computer sits around with little to do:

- Do you use hard copy often? Once data or text is printed on paper, managing it becomes a manual process. This is terribly inefficient, not to mention a waste of paper. Traditional-style corporate managers often fall into this trap.

- Do you sort data or count lines and objects manually? Most operating environments, especially Linux, provide tools to perform these tasks much faster than you can.

- How do you find files on the system? Do you locate them by browsing your directories one by one? Or do you create a list of your files and scan it with an editor or browsing tool? The Linux commands *find, grep,* and *locate* can be a powerful combination in these situations.

- When trying to find a particular item in a file, do you scan the file manually, relying on your eyes to lead you to the right place? Or do you employ a browser or editor "search" command to let the system do the scanning for you?

- Do you use a history mechanism if your command interpreter provides one? A history mechanism allows you to invoke previous commands using a shorthand method. The Linux shells *csh* and *bash* are especially good in this regard.

- If you have a system with multiple-window capability, do you use only one window at a time? You benefit by opening two or more windows simultaneously. You can target one window as the space in which you work (edit, compile, etc.) The other becomes your test space. Even better, some Linux window managers offer multiple-desktop capabilities. These allow you to manage several windows as a group. The resulting efficiency gains are often dramatic.

- How often do you use cut-and-paste facilities? If you find yourself frequently entering long strings manually, you're probably not making the most of these. One person I know keeps a window on the screen containing frequently used strings. He cuts the strings from the window and then pastes them in other windows as he needs them, saving himself much typing.

- Does the command interpreter you use provide command and/ or file completion capabilities? Do you use these capabilities to accelerate your input, saving you from having to enter many additional keystrokes?

The use of software leverage through increased automation can result in huge productivity gains. I once worked at a place where a significant part of the job involved culling small amounts of information from a diverse collection of sources. In a study we conducted, we observed that each individual was spending as many as 20 hours a week locating the necessary data. This number did not include the time spent reading and verifying the information once it had been located either. A simple tool was written to index information from the wide variety of sources for rapid retrieval. The payoff? People using the tool spent as few as three hours a week locating the same data that couldn't be found in more than 15 hours before. Office productivity soared. Everyone was excited. What was once a cumbersome research job was now a painless, highly interactive series of queries carried out by machines. This freed up our time to tackle tougher problems that the machines could not handle.

Every time you automate a task, you experience the same kind of leverage that my aunt enjoyed when she found others to sell Tupperware for her. Each command procedure and each program you invoke sends your computer off on a wild spree to complete a task. Instead of convincing people to do your bidding, you direct a well-tuned machine to carry out certain procedures according to instructions you specify. The faster the machine, the bigger the leverage. With next year's machine, your leverage will have an even greater impact. And, of course, a machine never gets tired or demands a larger percentage of the profits.

In the first part of this chapter we explored some principles concerning the use of leverage, both from a general standpoint and specifically with respect to how leverage applies to software. We have seen how it is important to become a "software scavenger" with an eye toward leveraging the work of others. After discussing the troublesome NIH syndrome, we stressed the value of sharing your work. Finally, we touched upon the obvious but often overlooked desirability of using the computer to leverage your time by automating daily tasks as much as possible.

Now that we have laid a foundation, it's time to build upon that foundation with another element of Unix, the shell script. Shell scripts capitalize on software leverage in interesting ways. They make it easy for both naïve and expert users to tap into the incredible potential found in Unix. Experienced Unix programmers use them religiously. You should, too.

Shell scripts bear some resemblance to other command interpreters and control mechanisms, such as batch files under MS-DOS and DCL command files under OpenVMS. Unlike these other implementations, however, Unix shell scripts exist in an environment ideally suited for indirect command execution. To highlight their significance, we include a special tenet in the Unix philosophy for them.

5.2   Tenet 7: Use shell scripts to increase leverage and portability

If you want to take full advantage of software leverage, you need learn how to use shell scripts effectively. We're not going to show you how to use them here. There are already plenty of books on the subject. Most will show you how to use them. Instead, we're going to focus on why you should use them.

Before entering into this discussion, I must caution you that many Unix and Linux kernel programmers disdain shell script programs. They believe that writing shell scripts is not the macho thing to do. Some even equate "experienced shell programmer" with "lightweight Linux programmer." My guess is that they're simply jealous because writing shell scripts doesn't involve much cerebral pain. Or perhaps it's because you cannot use shell scripts in the kernel. Maybe someone will write a Linux kernel that will allow the use of shell scripts in the kernel itself someday. Then they, too, can more fully appreciate the benefits of software leverage.

In examining the case for shell scripts, you may get the impression that the author is anti-C; that is, programs should never be written in a portable language like C anymore. If so, you're missing the point. There are times when writing a program in C instead of the shell makes perfect sense. But those times occur much less often than one might suspect.

Similarly, because of all of the hype surrounding object-oriented languages and tools these days, it's easy to fall into the trap of bypassing the shell and writing all software in a popular language such as Java. While in many ways Java is an excellent language, especially with respect to code reuse, it is still a compiled language (i.e., you must compile a Java program from the source code before the Java run-time engine can interpret it). This section will make you aware of the shell alternative to Java, if it doesn't change your mind altogether.

5.2.1   Shell scripts give you awesome leverage

Shell scripts consist of one or more statements that specify native or interpreted programs and other shell scripts to execute. They run these programs indirectly by loading each command into memory and executing it. Depending on the kind of statement, the top-level shell program may or may not choose to wait for individual commands to complete. The executed commands have been compiled from as many as a hundred, a thousand, or even a hundred thousand lines of C source code, most of which you did not write. Someone else took the time to code and debug those programs. Your shell script is merely the beneficiary, and it uses those lines of code to good advantage. Although you have expended comparatively little effort on your part, you gain the benefit of as many as a million or more lines of code. Now that's leverage.

In the multilevel marketing of plastic housewares, the trick is to get other people to do much of the work for you. You're trying to create a situation where someone else sows and you reap part of the reward. Shell scripts provide that opportunity. They give you the chance to incorporate the efforts of others to meet your goals. You don't write most of the code used in a shell script because someone else has already done it for you.

Let's look at an example. Suppose you wanted a command to list the names of a system's users on a single line. To make it more interesting, let's separate each user's name by commas and display each name only once, no matter how many sessions a user may have opened on the system. This is how our command might look as a shell script written in the *bash* shell, a popular Linux command interpreter:

```
echo `who | awk '{print $1}' | sort | uniq` | sed 's/ /, /g
```

Although this shell script consists of a single line, it invokes six different executables: *echo, who, awk, sort, uniq,* and *sed.* These commands are run simultaneously in a kind of series-parallel progression. Except for the *who* command, which starts the sequence, each command receives its data from the previous command in the series and sends its output to the next command in the series. Several pipes, denoted by ' | ' characters, manage the data transfer. The final command in the sequence, *sed,* sends its output to the user's terminal.

Each command works with the others synergistically to produce the final output. The *who* command produces a columnar list of the users on the system. It feeds this to *awk* via the pipe mechanism. The first column in the output from *who* contains the names of the users. The *awk* command saves this column and throws away the rest of the data generated by *who.* The list of users is then sent to *sort,* which places them in alphabetical order. The *uniq* command discards any duplicate names caused by users who may have logged in to several sessions at once.

Now we have a sorted list of names, separated by "newlines," the Linux end-of-line or line-feed character. This list is sent to the *echo* command via a "back-quoting" mechanism that places the output of the previous commands on the *echo* command line. The *bash* shell's semantics here dictate that single spaces replace all newlines. Finally, our string of user names separated by spaces is sent to the *sed* command, and the spaces are converted to commas.

While this might seem quite amazing if you have never seen a Linux system before, it is a typical Linux-style command execution. It is not unusual to invoke multiple commands from a single command line in a shell script.

How much code was executed here? The shell script writer took less than a minute to write the script. Others wrote the commands invoked by the script. Under one version of Linux available today, the six commands used contain the following numbers of source code lines:

echo	177
who	755
awk	3,412
sort	2,614
uniq	302
sed	2,093
Total:	9,353

One line in this shell script executes the equivalent of 9,535 lines of source code! Although this is not an extraordinary number, this many lines are enough to prove our point. We have increased our power by a factor of 9,353 to 1. Again, we have leverage.

This was a simple example of a shell script. Some shell scripts today span several dozen pages containing hundreds of command lines. When you account for the C code behind each executable, the numbers really start to add up. The resulting leverage boggles the mind. As we shall see later, this phenomenon even impressed Albert Einstein.

5.2.2 Shell scripts leverage your time, too

Shell scripts have an intrinsic advantage in that they are interpreted rather than compiled. In a standard C-language development environment, the sequence of events goes like this:

```
THINK-EDIT-COMPILE-TEST
```

The shell script developer's environment is one step shorter:

```
THINK-EDIT-TEST
```

The shell script developer bypasses the COMPILE step. This may not seem like a big win given today's highly optimized compilers. Used with speedy RISC processors, such compilers can turn source code into binaries in the blink of an eye. But today's applications are rarely single files that exist by themselves. They're usually part of large build environments that lean toward complexity. What used to take a few seconds to compile on a fast machine may now take a minute or more because of increasing levels of integration. Larger programs can take several minutes or more. Complete operating systems and their related commands can require hours to build.

In skipping the compilation step, the script writers remain focused on the development effort. They don't need to go for coffee or read mail while waiting for the command build to complete. Proceeding immediately from EDIT to TEST, they don't have time to lose their train of thought while waiting for the compiler to finish. This greatly accelerates the software development process.

One key point to consider is execution time versus compilation time. Many smaller applications (remember that we're talking about Unix/Linux here) can accomplish their tasks in a few seconds or so. If the compilation takes significantly longer than that, then using a script may be desirable. On the other hand, if a script may take several hours to run where a compiled program would execute the same in several minutes, then by all means write a C program. Just be sure that you have carefully considered whether there might be a way to save time by scripting various components.

Alas, there is an advantage the C programmer has over the shell script author—namely, an enhanced set of tools for debugging. While developers have created a respectable amount of diagnostic software for the C language, the choices of debugging tools for script writers are severely limited. To date no full-featured debugger for shell scripts has emerged. Shell script writers must still rely on primitive mechanisms such as *sh -x* to display the names of the commands as they execute. Convenient breakpoint facilities are nonexistent. Examining variables is a tedious process. One could argue that, given the ease of shell programming, more comprehensive debugging facilities are unnecessary. I suspect that most shell script writers would disagree.

What about large IDEs such as Microsoft's Visual Studio or Borland's JBuilder? Don't they provide superior debugging and editing facilities? Yes, they do. They are very good at hiding the complexities of the underlying technology from the developer. Sometimes that's a good thing. But frequently the complaint is that when things go wrong, one still has to look underneath the covers to see what the IDE has done. The pretty outer shell that had made the language easier to use now becomes the developer's nemesis as he or she tries to figure out what went wrong behind the scenes.

Shell scripts, on the other hand, keep things very visible. Everything they do is right there in front of you. Nothing is hidden behind dropdown menus in a slick GUI. The irony is that shell scripts are more visual than the so-called visual products.

5.2.3   Shell scripts are more portable than C

A sure way to leverage your software is to make it portable. Earlier we learned that it is important that you share your software with others. Any program moved easily from one platform to another is likely to be used by many people. The more people using your software, the greater the leverage.

In the Linux environment, shell scripts generally represent the highest level of portability. Most scripts that work on one Linux system are likely to work on another with little or no modification. Since they are interpreted, it is not necessary to compile them or otherwise transform them for use. It is possible to make a shell script nonportable by design, but such instances are rare and are usually not encouraged.

Shell scripts also tend to lack the stigma of "ownership" commonly associated with C source code. People rarely become protective of them. Since they are plainly visible to everyone, no one considers it his or her corporate duty to protect their contents. Still, a measure of caution is in order here. Copyright laws in the United States and other countries provide protection for shell scripts. Whether one would want to copyright a shell script is a matter for the lawyers.

5.2.4   Resist the desire to rewrite shell scripts in C

The chapter on portability urged you not to rewrite shell scripts in C because next year's machine will make them run faster. Since shell scripts are usually highly portable, moving them to Next Year's Machine generally involves virtually no effort. You copy them to the new machine and they run. Period. No mess, no fuss.

Unfortunately, the ability to leave well enough alone is not a virtue typical of programmers. If programmers can find a spare moment to tinker with a shell script, you can bet that they will (1) add some new features to it, (2) attempt to make it run faster by refining the script itself, or (3) try to improve its performance by rewriting part or most of it in C. Can you guess which is most tempting?

The desire to rewrite shell scripts in C stems from the belief that C programs run faster than shell scripts. This eats away at the programmer's desire for a neat, orderly world where everything is well tuned and highly efficient. It's an ego thing. He knows he could have written it in C, and it would have run faster from the beginning. For whatever reason, he didn't. Guilt sets in. If you ask him why he chose to write a program as a shell script, he'll mumble something like, "It was all I had time for." He'll follow this excuse with a promise that, when he gets more time, he will rewrite in C.

It's time to get over it. It's doubtful that he will ever get the chance. Any programmer worth his salary will be much too busy to go back and rewrite a shell script that already works well enough to meet the needs of its users. Life is much too short for that.

Furthermore, the belief that C programs run faster than shell scripts bears some scrutiny. In the first place, a shell script invokes C programs to accomplish its task. Once the C programs are loaded for execution, "pure" C programs enjoy no performance advantage over those called from within a script. Most Linux systems today have tuned the command execution routines so well that the time required to load a program for execution is relatively small compared with the time to perform the complete task.

If you really want your shell scripts to run quickly, then you must look into different ways of solving a problem. Too often, users and programmers fall into a rut, saying that's the way I've always done it, and that's the way I'll always do it. Instead, you need to train yourself to overlook the obvious approaches and find techniques that use the available resources in novel ways.

By way of example, let's look at a situation I ran into a few years ago. I was working in an environment where I received between 50 and 100 pieces of e-mail each day, or about 300 per week. Although I could read and delete some messages, I had to save others for future reference. It wasn't long before I had over 2,000 mail messages spread across 100 directories on my Unix system. Accessing the right one quickly was becoming difficult.

The obvious solution would be to use the Unix *grep* command to locate each message based on searching its contents for a particular text string. The problem with this approach was that it was very time consuming, even for a fast program like *grep*. I needed something better.

After a few false starts, I came up with the idea of indexing all of the mail messages. I wrote a shell script that did a *grep* on every file in the directories using all possible text strings. In effect, the index I created had "pre-grep'ed" the files. When I wanted to find a mail message, I looked in the index for a text string contained in the message, such as the author or the subject. The index would return a pointer to the file or files containing the string. This approach turned out to be far more efficient than running *grep* every time to find a message, even though it uses a shell script.

This approach worked out so well that I passed the idea on to a co-worker who implemented it on a much larger scale. Within a couple of months, he was using the same technique to index huge numbers of files on our systems. He refined the shell scripts until they could locate a string in several hundred megabytes of text in a few seconds—on our slowest machine. The application worked so well that most people did not believe that it was written as a shell script.

While *grep* may be much faster than many commands run from a shell script, by using a different approach it is possible to produce a shell script with remarkably higher performance than *grep* alone. It's just a matter of looking at the problem from a new angle.

In this chapter we have explored the value of leverage. We have seen that leverage can be an especially powerful idea when applied to software. Like any form of compounding, software leverage produces extensive effects for small amounts of effort. Each small program is a seed that becomes a mighty oak when sown.

Shell scripts remain an optimum choice for enhancing software leverage. They allow you to take the work of others and use it to your advantage. Even if you have never written a sort routine, you can have a sort routine written by an expert at your disposal. This kind of approach makes everyone a winner, even those who cannot program their way out of a paper bag.

One of the strengths of the Unix philosophy is its emphasis on a plethora of tiny commands. The shell script is a way to unify them into a powerful whole, thereby giving even inexperienced programmers the ability to perform difficult tasks with ease. Using shell scripts, you can stand on the shoulders of giants, who themselves are standing upon the shoulders of giants, ad infinitum. Now that's leverage!

Albert Einstein once said, "I have only seen two miracles in my life, nuclear fusion and *compound interest*" (italics added). For all of his wonderful theories, these two ideas evidently impressed him most. He understood that a small amount of something, multiplied repeatedly, can grow to miraculous proportions. It took a keen mind like his to recognize the power in this simple idea.

On the other hand, maybe his wife used to sell Tupperware.

6

The Perils of Interactive Programs

So Volkswagen was right. Small really is beautiful. Power rests not with the big and strong, but with the small and capable. You only have to witness the number of compact cars on the American landscape today to realize that millions of people have arrived at the same conclusion. And Volkswagen did it again with the "retro" bug. Small is "in." Forever "in."

This fondness for the diminutive doesn't stop with cars, either. People are discovering that little things generally have tremendous advantages over their larger counterparts. Paperback books have long outsold hardcover editions, partly because they're less expensive and partly because they're easier to take everywhere. Wristwatches have replaced pocket watches because of their reduced size and greater portability. Technological advances have given today's miniature electronic components more capability than much larger components in the past. Sales of pocket TVs, palmtop computers, and hand-held remote controls are skyrocketing. Even today's nuclear weapons are considerably smaller than the ones dropped on Japan during World War II, yet they possess substantially more destructive power.

We owe much of this shrinking universe to superior technology. It takes highly advanced technology to reduce a mainframe computer to a microchip small enough to fit in one's hand. Without the miniaturization afforded by high-density microprocessors, many of today's products would be too cumbersome to be useful.

Still, it requires some level of user sophistication to be able to use these high-technology wonders. It seems as if the smaller and more advanced a device is, the more a user must know to be able to use it.

One example is the evolution of microwave ovens for the home. Early versions employed a start button and a plain knob for the timer. Then, as computer chip prices fell, it became chic to produce ovens that were programmable. These ovens were considerably more intelligent, but they also required more intelligent users to be able to take advantage of their advanced features.

Another way to look at it is that children don't learn how to write first with an ultrafine marker. They start with big, fat crayons. Why? Crayons require the child to hold on with whatever grip he or she can manage. Writing with a razor tip marker requires a greater level of manual dexterity. A child doesn't reach this skill level until several years after first picking up the crayon.

From these examples we can draw a couple of conclusions. First, small things don't interface well with people. While micro technology may be making things smaller, people aren't getting any smaller. Once a certain point of reduction is reached, people lose the ability to deal with things directly. They must resort to tools that enhance their normal senses. For instance, a watch-maker doesn't use the naked eye to scrutinize the tiny parts inside a fine Swiss watch. He must resort to using magnifying lenses that allow him to see the components. Similarly, in today's semiconductor manufacturing facilities, microscopes are used to spot defects in integrated circuits packing millions of transistors per square inch.

The human senses function only within narrow limits. Sounds can be too soft or too loud to be heard. There are light waves at frequencies lower than the eye can perceive. With our sense of smell we can distinguish among per-fume varieties or gag from the stench of a skunk, but we have trouble distinguishing between the scents of *two* skunks.

As technology causes things to grow smaller, eventually they reach a point where our senses can no longer perceive them. Then a special interface is required for human beings to be able to deal with them. As computers become increasingly sophisticated, the gap between what exists and what the senses perceive widens. The distance between the software carrying out a given task and its user interface becomes an ever-widening void.

The second conclusion we can draw about small things is that, while they do not interface well with people, they tend to interface well with each other. Their small size gives them tremendous flexibility. They are readily suited for integration in many situations.

Consider this example: The next time you see a moving van in your neighborhood, watch how the workers load the customer's belongings. If they're putting an automobile on the van, it goes on first. Then they decide where the next largest pieces go. They follow these with the mid-sized pieces and then the small pieces. The sequence is obvious. But what is really happen-ing is a demonstration that smaller things combine with each other in myriad ways to accomplish a task. While you have some flexibility in the placement of the smaller pieces, the larger ones afford fewer placement choices.

What would happen if you had only small pieces? You would achieve maximum flexibility. This flexibility comes with a price, though. The more small pieces you have, the harder it is for people to deal with them. Managing them becomes a serious problem.

Similarly, in the world of computer software, having many small pro-grams and modules gives you the greatest ability to adapt to the environment. Unfortunately, as the modules get smaller, the issue arises of interfacing with the user. The more modules there are, the greater the complexity in dealing with them.

This presents a dilemma for the software designer. He wants maximum flexibility for his application, so he constructs it from a collection of small modules. Yet he is also bound by the requirement that his software be easy to use. People have difficulty dealing with too many small modules.

Unix takes a different approach to resolving this issue. Most other systems try to bridge the ever-widening gap between the user and the module performing the task with a piece of software known as a captive user interface (CUI). Unix developers, on the other hand, recognize that this gap is ever widening. Instead of linking the user and the underlying modules via a mass of "spaghetti" code, they work away at the gap with small chunks or layers.

Since we've just said that Unix and other operating systems diverge on this point, you may suspect that there is an underlying rationale for this. The answer comes from the next tenet of the Unix philosophy.

6.1   Tenet 8: Avoid captive user interfaces

Before we begin a discussion of the reasons for avoiding CUIs, we first need to define them. A CUI is a style of interaction with an application that exists outside the scope of the highest-level command interpreter present on the system. Once you invoke an application from the command interpreter, it is not possible to communicate with the command interpreter until the application exits. You are, in effect, held captive within the user interface of the application until you take actions that cause it to release you.

Let's clarify this with an example. Suppose you have two programs, one that lists the contents of your electronic mailbox and another that searches for a text string in files. If the mail and search programs use CUIs, your interaction might look something like this:

`$ mail`	Invoke the *mail* program from the command line.
`MAIL>dir`	Show the contents of the mailbox.
`MAIL>exit`	Exit the *mail* program. Return to command interpreter level.
`$ search`	Invoke the *search* program.
`SEARCH>find jack *.txt`	Perform the search.
`SEARCH>exit`	Exit the *search* program.
	:
	::
`$`	We're back at the command interpreter level.

Notice the flow between the levels here. First, invoking the *mail* command places you inside its own input interpreter. It forces you to interact with its command parser. The parser has a command set different from that of the command interpreter that called it. Second, to execute the *search* command, you must first leave the *mail* command by entering an *exit* command. You then called the *search* command from the main command interpreter. Once you're inside the *search* application, you must then interact with another command interpreter. This interpreter behaves differently from both the main command interpreter and the *mail* command's interpreter. The only similarity is that it requires you to enter an *exit* command to end it.

You can see that there are obvious disadvantages with this approach. You must become familiar with three different command interpreters, each with its own interaction language. This may not sound too difficult on a small scale, but it can become prohibitive very quickly on a system that has hundreds of applications. Also, while executing a command, you cannot do anything else until you exit from it. Suppose, for instance, that in responding to a letter in your mailbox, you needed to include some text from another file but you forget which one. You would have to exit from the *mail* command, do the search, and then return to the *mail* command. At that point you probably will have forgotten your context in the *mail* application.

So much for the obvious drawbacks. The reasons Unix devotees eschew captive user interfaces are not so obvious. Before we explore these, however, let's contrast this CUI with a Unix-style "noncaptive" interface:

`shs>can`	The *scan* command lists the contents of a mail folder.
	:
	::
`sh>grep jack *.txt`	The *grep* command searches for the string "jack" in all files having names ending in ".txt".

Notice that the Unix user invokes all commands at the shell prompt or main command interpreter level. Each command completes its task, and control returns to the shell prompt. It is not necessary to exit from each command individually by typing "exit." The user needs to learn only one language—that of the shell, the Unix command interpreter.

The cynic might point out that the user still must learn the order or parameters to be supplied for each command invocation. This is true. But with the CUI, the user must first recall which command to run, then which subcommand to invoke from its CUI. Therefore, there is nearly twice as much to remember. It is not surprising, then, that systems that employ CUIs often must provide highly developed help systems to guide users through the choices. On the other hand, most Unix users get by quite well without complex help systems. Unix commands often return simple messages listing the required parameters and their usage if the user enters an incorrect one.

Thus far, we've defined CUIs and touched upon some of their glaring deficiencies. The real reasons that Unix users avoid them, though, run much deeper. They have to do with the way commands interact with each other. In the Unix environment, no command exists in isolation. Commands interact with each other at various times. CUIs interfere with the ability of multiple commands to make this happen. Multiple command interaction is a key Unix concept.

6.1.1 CUIs assume that the user is human

Producers of CUIs base their designs on the premise that a person is sitting at the keyboard. They expect the person to enter responses to the prompts provided by the application. The application then performs calculations or carries out various tasks.

The problem, however, is that even the fastest human being is slower than the average computer. The computer can conduct operations at lightning speed, and it doesn't get tired or take breaks. As stated earlier, people function only within a narrow range. For example, even the speediest typists do not type much more than 80 words per minute. Most CUIs eventually reach a point where the user must respond to a prompt. Then even the fastest supercomputer is little more effective than the lowliest PC. Virtually all PCs capture text typed by users without the least bit of strain. As long as a system is constrained to operate within the limits imposed by human beings, it cannot function at its maximum potential.

I first became aware of this phenomenon when confronted with a window system running on a very fast workstation. Back in the days before PCs, most people were accustomed to scanning text files on a terminal. Terminals usually allowed you to stop and start the displayed output by pressing a <^S>/<^Q> combination or a "HOLD SCREEN" key. At modem speeds of 9,600 bps or lower, most people could control the scrolling rate without any trouble. Today's window systems, however, have no artificial limit such as the communications speed to control the rate at which the system displays text. The user is entirely at the mercy of the CPU and its I/O capabilities. When left to its own devices, so to speak, the computer can display text considerably faster than anyone can deal with it by entering <^S>. This situation will worsen in the future as large cache memories and machines in the multi-gigahertz speed range become common.

Because of the limitations we humans impose on computers, any system that must wait for user input can operate only as fast as the person sitting at the keyboard. In other words, not very fast at all.

Typical Unix commands strive to perform their tasks entirely without human intervention. Most only prompt the user when they are about to take some potentially irreversible action such as "repairing" a file system by deleting files. As a result, Unix commands always run at maximum speed. This is part of the reason a system designed for portability instead of efficiency still performs well. It recognizes that the weakest link, performancewise, in many man-machine interactions is not the machine.

6.1.2   CUI command parsers are often big and ugly to write

A parser reads the user's input and translates it into a form that the application software can understand. It has to read correctly everything a user might conceivably (and inconceivably!) type. This causes the typical command parser to grow to gargantuan proportions. Sometimes the command parser will require more programming than the application's main task.

Consider this example. Suppose you had a program for formatting a hard disk. Since the potential for data loss is great, you might consider it "user friendly" to ask the user whether he really wants to wipe out everything on the disk:

```
FORMAT V1.0 Rev.A

About to format drive C:

Formatting will destroy all files on the disk!

Begin format? <y|N>
```

The number of potential user responses to a prompt like this one is staggering. First, if the user wants to go ahead with the format, he may enter Y, y, Yes, YES, or various combinations in between. Similarly, if he is sure that he doesn't want to proceed, he may enter N, n, no, or NO. These responses are fairly easy to parse.

The complexity begins when the user isn't quite sure what he or she wants to do. An unsophisticated user might enter "help" in the hope of getting more general information about formatting. A more experienced user could enter "?" to obtain a list of formatting options. Still other users might try to break out of the formatting command altogether by forcing it to exit by means of one or more interrupt characters. Some of these may cause the formatter application to exit ungracefully or even terminate the user's login session.

To handle such reactions, a command parser must be large and highly sophisticated, a "tunnel through solid rock" according to Chris Crawford, (see Chapter 9). You can imagine how large a parser would be if the application required multiple prompts. The amount of code would comprise the bulk of the application.

The Unix programmer deals with the user interface by avoiding it (i.e., the typical Unix application doesn't have a command parser). Instead, it expects its operating parameters to be entered on the command line when invoking the command. This eliminates most of the possibilities described above, especially the less graceful ones. For those commands that have many command line options—a cautionary sign to begin with—Unix provides standard library routines for weeding out bad user input. This results in significantly smaller application programs.

Another approach here would be to use a dialog box with a GUI. This can be especially useful with commands, such as FORMAT, that have potentially disastrous effects. One doesn't want to wipe clean one's hard drive because of a poorly chosen letter. A GUI can be used in this case to get users to slow down and think about what they're doing.

While GUIs can be wonderful for guiding users through tunnels in solid rock, however, they don't let you connect the tunnels together very well. Solid rocks, especially BIG solid rocks, are such time-consuming things to drill through. We'll explore this in more detail later.

6.1.3   CUIs tend to adopt a big is beautiful approach

Many CUIs employ menus to restrict the user to a limited set of choices. This sounds good in theory. But for some unknown reason, CUI designers are seldom satisfied with a simple menu having, say, five items. They usually add menu items that invoke "submenus" to expand the number of options. It's as if they're thinking, "Hey! I went to all this trouble to design this menu system;

I may as well use it for something." So "creeping featurism" takes precedence over brevity.

The marketing arm of the computer industry must also share some blame. The constant push for "features, Features, FEATURES!" forces software designers to expand the number of menu choices without regard to whether the features are truly helpful or even make sense at all. From a salesperson's point of view, it's not enough to make the application better. It must look better. If a program sells well with 5 menu choices, then one with 10 will sell even better. It doesn't matter that the additional complexity may alienate much of the target market.

There are technical reasons, too, for avoiding CUIs and their "big is beautiful" approach. As CUIs grow in complexity, they need an ever-increasing number of system resources. Memory requirements explode upward. More disk space must be purchased. Network and I/O bandwidth becomes an issue. Consequently, computer hardware vendors love CUIs.

6.1.4   Programs with CUIs are hard to combine with other programs

One strength of Unix is the way its programs interact with each other so effectively. Programs with CUIs, because they assume that the user is human, do not interface well with other programs. Software designed for communicating with other software is usually much more flexible than the software designed to communicate with people.

Do you remember the example of workers loading a moving van? We said that the large pieces did not fit well with each other and it was the small pieces that provided the most flexibility. Similarly, programmers find it difficult to connect programs having CUIs to each other because of their size. CUIs tend to result in huge programs. Large programs, like large pieces of furniture, are not very portable. Movers don't say, "Hand me that piano, will ya?" any more than programmers move complex, monolithic applications from one platform to another overnight.

CUI programs' inability to combine with other programs causes them to grow to massive proportions. Since the programmer cannot rely on interfacing easily with other programs on the system to obtain the required capabilities, he must build new features into the program itself. This deadly spiral feeds on itself: The more features built into the CUI program, the larger it becomes. The larger it becomes, the greater the difficulty in interfacing it with other programs. As it gets harder to interface with other programs, the CUI program itself must incorporate more features.

6.1.5 CUIs do not scale well

CUIs tend to work well when dealing with only a few instances. By limiting choices, they can make it easier for an inexperienced user to accomplish complex tasks. As long as there are not too many instances, the user is usually content to respond to the prompts. The number of prompts can become unwieldy, however, when one must respond to several hundred of them.

A popular program (a shell script, really) provided by many Unix system vendors is *adduser*. It allows the system administrator to add a new user account to the system via a "user-friendly" CUI. Most of the time it works well. The problem with *adduser* becomes evident when you must add, say, several thousand users at once.

Once a university had decided to change from another OS to Unix. Several thousand user accounts were to be transferred to the new system. It didn't take long for the system administrators to realize that running *adduser* that many times wasn't going to cut it. They ultimately settled on a solution that involved moving the user account files from the old system to the Unix system. Then they wrote a shell script to convert them into files resembling the Unix password file. The irony was that the shell script written to do the conversion was shorter than *adduser*.

6.1.6 Most important, CUIs do not take advantage of software leverage

Because CUI programs expect to communicate with a human being at some point, it is very difficult to incorporate them into shell scripts. It takes many lines in a shell script to carry on the kinds of dialogs that CUIs require. These dialogs can be so cumbersome to write in a shell script that programmers often resort to small user interface programs to conduct yes-no queries and obtain other responses from the user.

Since CUIs hinder interaction with other programs, they are typically used only for their original purpose and not much else. Although you might suggest that this is simply a case of "doing one thing well," a CUI differs from small Unix commands in that it exists as an application unto itself. It doesn't offer the same mix-and-match, plug-and-play features of its Unix counterparts. It yields very little in terms of software leverage as a result.

Without software leverage, CUI programs cannot multiply their effects—and the effects of their developers—on the computer world. Although a CUI program may gain an early following because of its novelty when it is released, it soon loses its appeal as the rest of the software world marches on. Software advances appear daily on the computer scene, and a few ideas cause major upheaval in each decade. The monolithic CUI program is simply incapable of adapting in such a rapidly evolving environment.

6.1.7   "Who cares about CUIs? Nobody types anymore."

Some of you may be wondering why there is so much discussion about CUIs in the first place. After all, aren't most user interfaces graphical these days? Why be concerned with typing things on the command line when you can view a list of check boxes and click on them with a mouse?

The short answer is that a GUI is simply a visual form of a CUI. Thus, it has the same characteristics as a CUI for the following reasons:

- *It assumes that the user is human.* The software designer expects that a physical user will be present to click on buttons and navigate menus. In some cases, steps are taken to slow the program down to better accommodate the user. Frequently, more effort is spent on making the user interface than on providing functional capabilities.

- *A GUI is often big and difficult to write.* Large IDEs such as Microsoft's Visual Basic and Borland's Jbuilder have ameliorated this problem somewhat. But these IDEs have problems of their own that we've explored elsewhere.

- *GUIs tend to adopt a big is beautiful approach.* If five options meet the need, then ten options meet the need even better. That's the rationale behind some office programs that have grown to gargantuan proportions. When you want to drive a couple of nails, you don't need to hire a construction company to come in with a team of laborers armed with nail guns.

- *It's difficult to combine GUI-based programs with other programs.* Unless the program has initially been designed to interface with another program, it won't interface well. In the Microsoft world, OLE and COM provide some of this connectivity. With most Unix and Linux com-

mands, such interfaces are unnecessary, as most of them already interface well with other programs.

- *GUIs do not scale well.* They have the same problem as CUIs, as
  shown by the *adduser* example. Clicking the mouse several times to
  perform an operation is easy. Clicking the mouse to perform the same
  operation thousands of times results in user frustration and a nag-
  ging sense that the computer is in charge instead of the other way
  around.

- *GUIs do not take advantage of software leverage.* It is extremely difficult
  to script operations performed only via a GUI. It is often necessary to
  resort to recorder-like programs that capture mouse and keyboard
  events. These provide an imperfect solution as situations often arise
  that require users to make decisions depending on the output produced
  by the program. Recorded scripts usually have little ability to deal with
  this situation. Those that can often require manual editing of the
  scripts, at which point you are once again operating in the scripter's
  world, not the GUI world.

Thus far in this chapter we have discussed how a CUI presents several
obstacles to a program's impact. CUIs make sense under certain circumstances, but they are the exception rather than the rule. Applications fare
much better if they are made of a collection of small components that communicate well with each other. It doesn't matter much if they do not interface
with human beings well. Ultimately a specialized program that, not surprisingly, is likely to be a CUI itself manages this interaction.

Programs that interact with each other are actually data filters. Each
gathers several bytes on its input stream, applies a filtering algorithm to
the data, and usually produces several bytes on its output system. We say
"usually produces" here, because not all programs send data to their output
stream. Depending on the data and the algorithms, some simply output
nothing.

The fact that programs filter data is significant. All computers and their
programs filter data. That's why we call them data processors. To process data
is to filter it.

If a program is a filter, then it ought to act like one; that is, it should
concentrate not on synthesizing data, but rather on selectively passing on
data that is presented to it. This is the essence of the next tenet of the Unix
philosophy.

6.2   Tenet 9: Make every program a filter

6.2.1   Every program written since the dawn of computing is a filter

Every program—no matter how simple or complex—accepts data in some form as its input and produces data in some form as its output. How the program filters the data presented to it depends on the algorithms contained therein.

Most people accept that programs such as text formatters and translators can be considered filters, but they have difficulty realizing that the same holds true for other programs not ordinarily regarded as filters. Take real-time data collection systems, for example. Typical ones sample analog-to-digital converters at periodic intervals to gather data for their input streams. They then select appropriate portions of this data and pass it to their output streams to user interfaces, other applications, or files for storage.

Do GUIs act as filters, too? Absolutely. GUIs normally process mouse button actions or keystrokes as "events." These events form the data stream fed to the input of applications on the screen under control of the window system. The applications, as filters, respond to these events, effecting changes on the display.

There is also the question of those programs that fail because of hardware errors. Suppose a program encounters a hard error in reading from a disk. Instead of getting data back when it tries to perform a read operation, it receives an error status. Most of the time it will filter the error indication and produce an error message to warn the user. In other words, an error status as input produces an error message as the output. The algorithm that figures out the error message to produce acts as a filter for the error condition as input.

6.2.2   Programs do not create data—people do

People commonly believe that their applications create data when applications are really incapable of manufacturing data. Data synthesis requires creativity. It requires an original source of information. A computer has no original source of information.

When a person uses a word processor, the text being written comes from that person's mind. The word processor functions solely as a tool for gathering ideas and storing them in a format easily housed and manipulated by the computer. It cannot write a book any more than a hammer and a box of nails can build a house. The more intelligent word processors—the ones we call "What You See Is What You Get" or WYSIWYG types—may do some filtering such as formatting and justification, but they still do not formulate the ideas in the first place.

Real-time programs that gather information about the world around us do not create data either. The data already exists. By extracting readings from their environments, the programs perform a process of selection. Only important data passes through the programs' filters so it can be saved.

The world is full of data created by people. This data would still exist if the computer had never been invented. The computer simply makes it possible to gather and filter the data more efficiently. Any "new" data produced is not new at all. The computer just gives us an opportunity to manage it in a different way. If the world were full of computers without any people, there would be no data.

6.2.3   Computers convert data from one form to another

An alternative view is that data, to be useful to most application programs, must be stored in a format that facilitates its manipulation. For example, the actions of a person depressing keys on the keyboard are of no value to a piece of software. However, once these actions are converted to a series of electronic impulses representing binary data, they suddenly take on a new life within the machine. Then the software can convert the data into a multitude of forms to serve any number of purposes.

An interesting side note here is that music is simply another kind of data. It has existed for centuries in one form or another. People have been playing stringed instruments for several thousand years. The piano, a stringed percussion instrument, has been around for many centuries. Player pianos contained rolls of paper with holes punched in them to "remember" the notes of songs. In recent years, though, the keyboard synthesizer has become the primary means to gather "data" produced by musicians moving their wrists and fingers. Once captured, the data is converted to MIDI files, the music industry's standard format for electronic music representation. As MIDI files, the data can be filtered in limitless ways, resulting in the production not only of piano tones but of other sounds beyond the capabilities of any natural acoustical instrument. In many ways, the music world's use of MIDI is still in its infancy. Future MIDI applications will bring us musical flights that will stretch the envelope of human audible perception. This will occur because of programs that can filter musical data in ways previously considered impossible. Most certainly, it will be computers that will modify and enhance MIDI data to produce new, creative sounds.

6.3   The Linux environment: Using programs as filters

You may be wondering what it means for a program to act as a filter. Linux programmers follow a set of unwritten rules that simplify designing software that behaves in this manner. To help clarify these rules, I've included several guidelines here. Before we discuss these, however, it is necessary to provide a short explanation of a concept in Linux called *stdio*.

When a program is invoked under Linux, it normally has three standard I/O channels open to it known as *stdin, stdout,* and *stderr,* hence the name *stdio.* What is connected to the other ends of these I/O channels depends on how the program was invoked. In the default case, *stdin* collects user input when the program is invoked, and *stdout* sends any program output to the user's display screen. Any output sent to *stderr* also appears on the display screen, but this data is normally considered "out of band" or error information.

An interesting feature of Linux *stdio* is that the devices connected to the I/O channels are not "hard-wired" to the program. At the time of invocation, the user may specify that data will originate from or be sent to places other than the user's terminal. For example, *stdin* may come from a file, another program via a Linux pipe, or even a satellite link to a system on the other side of the world. Similarly, if the user wanted to save *stdout* in a file for later perusal, he or she could direct the Linux shell to place the output there. This provides for enormous flexibility with respect to the source and destination of the data.

How Linux programmers deal with *stdio* has a significant impact on the ability of a program to function as a filter. If the program is written correctly, then all the adaptability of *stdio* can be used. Otherwise, the user is likely to be locked within a CUI. The key, then, is to write the software so that it employs *stdio.* Here are three important guidelines:

1.   Use stdin for data input

Programs that obtain their input from *stdin* assume that their data could come from anywhere. Indeed it could. By avoiding "hard-wiring" the input channel, you make it easy for the user to specify where the input will come from when invoking the program. Its source could be the keyboard, a file, another Linux program, or even a CUI.

2.   Use stdout for data output

As *stdin* usage allows your program to accept input data from anywhere, the use of *stdout* allows your program's output to be sent anywhere. "Anywhere" here may mean the user's screen, a file, a printer, or even a digital speech synthesizer. The choice is up to the user, and it can be whatever is appropriate when the program is run.

3.   Use stderr for out-of-band information

Error messages and other warnings should be sent to the user via *stderr.* They should never be part of the data stream sent to *stdout.* One reason for this is that the user may choose to capture error messages in a separate file or perhaps view them on the terminal immediately. Sending error messages on the same I/O channel as *stdout* can cause confusion further down the line. Remember that Linux commands are seldom used alone.

Notice how this approach differs from that of other operating systems. Applications running on most other systems tend to hard-wire everything. They assume that there will always be a user sitting at the keyboard. They may ask the user if he or she would like to send the output to a file, but they seldom offer the individual this choice unless a conscious effort was made to include this capability.

Hard-wiring the I/O implies that you know all possible users for your program. This is sheer egotism. In an earlier chapter we stressed that everyone is on a learning curve. No one can predict how his or her software will always be used. The best you can do is make the interface to your programs flexible enough to deal with as many eventualities as exist today. Beyond that, let tomorrow take care of tomorrow.

After having spent many years in a software engineering environment, I once took a position in a telephone support center where I answered customer questions about software—in many cases my software. It was most enlightening to speak with customers who depended on the software to do their jobs. I listened intently to hundreds of them tell stories of how they were doing the unbelievable with my software. My most common reaction was, "It wasn't meant to do that!"

Recent network security break-ins have made it painfully clear that malicious users often attempt to do things that the software was never intended to do. These break-ins usually result from exploitation of buffer overflows and other programming errors that leave systems vulnerable. While the programmer may have intended for a program operate in a certain way, a system cracker will often invent strange and not-so-wonderful ways to use it to gain unauthorized access.

You never know what people are going to do with your software. Never, ever assume that they will use it solely for the purpose you intended. You may think that you're writing a simple sort program, a word processor, or a file compression routine. You'll soon discover that someone is using the sort program to translate ASCII to EBCDIC, the word processor has become a public access bulletin board, and the file compression routine is being used to digitize *Gone with the Wind* for downloading over the local cable TV system.

It's easier to avoid developing programs with CUIs if you keep in mind that all programs are filters. When you assume that the receptacle of a program's data flow might be another program instead of a human being, you eliminate those biases we all have in trying to make an application user friendly. You stop thinking in terms of menu choices and start looking at the possible places your data may eventually wind up. Try not to focus inward on what your program can do. Look instead at where your program may go. You'll then begin to see the much larger picture of which your program is a part.

When regarding programs as filters, software designers break their applications down into collections of smaller programs, each of which performs a function of the application. Not only do these small programs communicate well with each other, they lack most of the bloat required to make their user interfaces "bulletproof." In a sense, their "users" are other programs. These programs will ultimately yield higher performance. They are not constrained by human capabilities that will fall behind when faster architectures are introduced in the future. And programs, as we said before, don't complain, develop attitudes, or call in sick.

Now, if we could just get the programmers not to complain, develop attitudes, or call in sick!

7

More Unix Philosophy: Ten Lesser Tenets

Thus far we have explored the tenets that form the core of the Unix philosophy. They are the bedrock upon which the Unix world sits. No one could strongly contest them and rightfully consider him or herself a "Unix person." To do so would invite suspicion by the Unix community (of which Linux is a part) that such a person lacked commitment to Unix and what it stands for.

Having pontificated on the dogmas of the Unix "religion" we are ready to embark upon some of its doctrines. Unix and Linux developers fight tooth and nail to preserve the integrity of the tenets covered up to this point. The precepts discussed here, on the other hand, fall in the "yeah, I kinda go along with that" category. Although not every Unix person will agree with the points in this chapter, the Unix community (and these days the Linux community) as a whole often aligns itself with them.

You will find that some items highlighted here are more concerned with how things should be done than why they should be done. I will try to provide some explanation for these, but be aware that some things are done for no other reason than that is the way they have always been done. Like established religion, Unix has its traditions, too. Linux is exhibiting the same characteristic in a kind of "same stuff, new wrapper" way.

Conspicuous by its absence is the topic of Open Source, the concept that most Linux "accidental revolutionaries" are dogmatic about. Because Open Source is so ingrained in Linux culture and had long ago become the rallying cry of pioneers such as Richard M. Stallman and others, it deserves more complete treatment than the lighter vignettes featured here. So we'll examine it in greater depth later.

It's not surprising that proponents of other operating systems have adopted some of these lesser tenets as well. Good ideas tend to spread in the computer world. Software developers on other systems have discovered Unix concepts that have shown merit in situations where they may not have seemed appropriate initially. They have incorporated these into their designs, sometimes resulting in systems and applications that have a Unix flavor.

7.1   Allow the user to tailor the environment

Many years ago I wrote *uwm*, a "window manager" or user interface for the X Window System. It provided the user capabilities that many people take for granted in today's window systems: the ability to move windows, resize them, change their stacking order, and so on. Well accepted in the marketplace, it went on to become "the standard window manager for X Version 10." It holds a little-known, but nonetheless legitimate place as the conceptual ancestor of popular window managers used with the X Window System today. Today's window managers borrow heavily from the original customization ideas found in *uwm* and its offspring.

One factor contributing to *uwm*'s success was an exclamation by Bob Scheifler during an early X Window System design meeting at MIT. Bob, a significant contributor to the overall design of X, was reviewing my thin specification for the "Unix Window Manager." Suddenly he blurted out, "Suppose I don't want the left mouse button to do that!" He went on to suggest that perhaps users might like to choose the function initiated by each mouse button.

Had I been a comic book character, you would have seen a light bulb suddenly appear over my head.

Uwm went on to break new ground in the area of "customizable" user interfaces. The X Window System made it possible for the user to choose a window manager. *Uwm* took customization a step further by permitting the user to choose the look, feel, and behavior of the window manager itself. Combinations of mouse movement, button clicks, colors, fonts, and even menu options could be decided by the user. So powerful was this notion that the developers of X Windows later designed a "resource manager" that provided user-level control of virtually every element of the display screen. This unprecedented amount of flexibility is still unmatched today, even by Microsoft's and Apple's desktop environments. Whereas those other systems give this flexibility to the developer, X Windows gives it to the user.

Earlier we said that the larger the investment a person has in something, the bigger the stake one has in its outcome. In observing how people used *uwm*, I found that if people are given the opportunity to tailor their environments, they will. Built-in flexibility invites the user to make an investment in learning how to get the most out of an application. As one becomes more comfortable with the environment one has tailored, the more resistant one becomes to using environments where such customization is difficult or impossible.

Much of the Linux environment today revolves around this axiom. People generally find it troublesome to use Linux at first because it is so flexible. The many choices overwhelm them. From the very start, Linux offers choices: multiple distributions, multiple window managers, multiple desktops, multiple file systems, and so on. You don't have to buy Linux from just one vendor. In fact, you don't even have to buy it at all. You can download it from one of the vendor sites for free.

Eventually, though, users find a way of using Linux that suits them. They choose a distribution and make an investment in learning how to take advantage of the many options. Once the investment reaches a certain level, it becomes very difficult to go back to other operating systems. They reach a point where their stake in Linux has grown so much that they would prefer to change what they don't like about it rather than leave it altogether.

Some people have criticized Linux, saying that it forces users to make a significant investment in learning its user interface before they can become productive with it. With Linux, they argue, it is too easy to shoot oneself in the foot. That may be true. But as Linux advocate Jon "maddog" Hall has asserted, it is better to let one shoot oneself in the foot than never to let one run at all.

7.2   Make operating system kernels small and lightweight

This is one hot topic with Unix purists and has been the subject of many debates over the years. The Unix kernel consists of those routines that, among other things, manage its memory subsystems and interface with its peripheral devices. It seems that any time people want higher application performance, the first thing they suggest is placing its runtime routines in the kernel. This reduces the number of context switches among running applications at the expense of making the kernel larger and incompatible with other Unix kernels.

During an early stage of the X Window System's development, a strong disagreement arose over whether higher performance would result from embedding part of the X server in the Unix kernel. (The X server is the part of the X Window System that captures user input from the mouse and keyboard and renders graphic objects on the screen.) The X server ran in user space (i.e., outside the kernel), making it relatively portable as window systems go.

The put-it-in-the-kernel camp advocated taking advantage of the smaller number of context switches between the kernel and user space to improve performance. The fact that the kernel was growing rapidly was of no consequence, they reasoned, since modern Unix systems had much more available memory compared to earlier ones. Therefore, there would still be plenty of memory left for the applications to run.

The user-space-for-everything crowd, on the other hand, argued that the X server would no longer be portable. Anyone modifying the X server would then need to be a Unix kernel guru, in addition to a graphics software developer. To remain a competent Unix kernel guru, one would have to forgo much interest in the graphics aspects of the X server. Thus, the X server would suffer.

How did the two camps resolve their differences? The system itself did it for them. After an apparently successful attempt to implant the X server into the kernel, testers discovered that a bug in the server would cause not only the window system to crash, but the entire operating system as well. Since a system crash is considered even less desirable than an X server crash, most X server implementations today reside solely in user space. Chalk one up for the user-space-for-everything crowd.

By avoiding the temptation to put everything in the kernel, it is easier to keep the kernel small and lightweight. Small and lightweight kernels speed the activation of tasks in user space by reducing the number of data structures copied or modified when starting a task. This ultimately makes it easier for collections of small programs that do one thing well to operate efficiently. Fast activation of small unifunctional programs is critical to Unix performance.

7.3   Use lowercase and keep it short

One thing people first notice about the Unix system is that everything is done in lower case. Instead of operating with the lock key on all the time, Unix users enter everything in lower case letters.

There are a couple of reasons for this. First, lowercase letters are much easier on the eyes. If a person must work with text for an extended period, it soon becomes apparent that viewing lower case text is much more pleasant than eyeing uppercase. Second, and perhaps more important, lowercase letters use ascenders and descenders, the tiny lines that extend above or below the baseline of text, such as those found on the letters "t," "g," and "p." They transmit intelligible cues that your eyes pick up on when you read. They make reading easier.

Case is also significant in Unix. For example, "MYFILE.TXT" and "MyFile.txt" do not represent the same file. Unix employs lowercase letters for frequently used commands and file names. The upper case is normally used to grab someone's attention. For example, naming a file "README" in a directory is a visual cue inviting the user to read the contents of the file before proceeding. Also, file names in directories are usually sorted alphabetically by the *ls* command, with capitalized names appearing before lowercase ones in a file list. This draws additional attention to the file.

While case sensitivity often causes much frustration for people who come to Unix after having used a case-insensitive operating system for a long time, they eventually adapt to it. Many even learn to like it.

Another quirk about Unix is that file names tend to be very short. Most frequently used command names are no more than two or three letters long. Terseness is golden here, and you will find such cryptic names as *ls, mv, cp,* and so on. Very long, multiword command names are often abbreviated to just the first letters of the words. For example, "parabolic anaerobic statistical table analyzer" reduces simply to "pasta."

The use of terse names is historical. Unix was originally developed on systems that had teletypes instead of CRT terminals. Typing on teletypes was accompanied by bzzzt-clunk sounds whenever one struck a key, and a fast teletypist could do about fifteen to twenty words per minute. Hence, shorter names for things were quite in vogue. The fact that most computer programmers back then didn't know how to type had nothing to do with it. (Well, maybe a little.)

Why do Linux users persist in using the shorter names today? Certainly today's PC keyboards can handle much higher speeds, so such brevity is no longer necessary. The reason is that shorter names allow you to cram much more on a command line. Remember that Linux shells have a pipe mechanism that allows you to string the output of one command into another on the command line.

This powerful feature is very popular with Linux users. They often string so many commands together on a single line that, if longer names were used, they would exceed the width of the window they're using. One solution to the problem is to keep the lengths of individual commands short so more of them will fit within smaller windows when you have several adjacent windows open on the screen.

Of course, you may be thinking "why bother?" Why not just click with the mouse and execute the commands directly? That works if you're using a command repeatedly. Remember, though, that a lot of the power of Unix and Linux comes from the ability to combine multiple commands dynamically to form new ones. This is not possible with most popular desktop environments today. The term WYSIWYG (what you see is what you get) is also WYSIATI (what you see is all there is). What you can click on is what you get and not much else. Attempts to provide graphical shells have produced cumbersome, inflexible user interfaces at best. And the use of "shortcuts" usually only shortens the time it takes to access a single command.[1]

7.4   Save trees

The term *Unix guru* probably came about because Unix is such an out-of-the-ordinary operating system. People who become experts in Unix tend to be regarded with both awe and suspicion: awe because they have mastered the mysteries of this fascinating computer environment, and suspicion because you wonder if this person might be slightly off his or her rocker to have devoted so much time to an operating system.

The first Unix guru I met was my boss early in my career at a small high-tech firm in southern New Hampshire. Besides preventing many of us from playing *Rogue* (a popular dungeon game) on company time, he also had responsibility for the daily management of our Unix system. Our Unix system ran on a Digital PDP-11/70, the same PDP-11/70 that had been running another operating system besides Unix before he arrived.

In those days, much programming was done in assembly language. The engineers in our department would spend hours writing and testing code that would be cross-assembled to run on a target machine of a different architecture. "Bit-twiddling" of this sort required paper listings. Lots of them. To debug a program, a person would generate an assembler listing and send it to our fastest line printer where it would appear as a stack of fanfold paper sometimes more than six inches thick. The more senior the programmer, the heftier the listing. If one wanted to gain respect in our shop, one simply had to generate longer listings. Obviously, anyone who could generate that much paper was certainly a hard worker, one worthy of significant compensation at salary review times. Management believed this myth, and we the engineers knew how to play it for all it was worth.

I was walking down the hall one day, laboring under a five-inch thick load of arboreal by-product, when my Unix guru boss stopped me and asked what I was doing with so much paper. "This is my program," I replied. I practically shoved the listing in his face as if to say, "Yes, I'm hard at work. Yessir!"

---

1.   Various desktop environments available on Linux allow you to execute multiple commands from a single shortcut. However, it's still a static capability without the ability to easily combine multiple commands dynamically. Whether it will continue to be static remains to be seen. One never knows what lurks in the minds of creative Linux people.

He grimaced. "You're killing too many trees. Come to my office."

He went straight to his terminal and proceeded to give me a lesson on Unix I'll never forget.

The point he made was this: Once you have printed your data on paper, you have largely lost the ability to manipulate it any further. Data on paper cannot be sorted, moved, filtered, transformed, modified, or anything else as easily as it can on a computer. You cannot search it at the touch of a key. It cannot be encrypted to protect sensitive information.

Do you remember earlier when we said that data that doesn't move is dead data? Paper poses a similar problem for your data. It's simply not possible to move paper data as fast as electronic bits stored on a computer. Therefore, paper data will always be "stale" compared with data kept on a computer. Just ask the publishers of the popular encyclopedias of the past. They are having fits today trying to sell encyclopedias in lovely leather-bound hardcover book form when people can get more timely information from the Internet.

With the growing popularity of fax machines, you may have observed that it is possible to transmit paper pages easily over telephone lines. But what happens to the information on the paper after transmission? It is locked into a medium that limits its usefulness.

Beware of paper. It is a death certificate for your data.

7.5   Silence is golden

No, we're not saying that Unix programmers shun multimedia. We're talking about so-called user-friendly programs that overstate the obvious or treat the user as though he or she were the software's best friend. Too many programmers believe that they're being helpful by addressing the user in a conversational tone. Unix is unusually dry in that it provides "just the facts, ma'am"—nothing more, nothing less.

Many Unix commands remain silent if they have received no input data or have no data to produce as output. This can be a bit disconcerting to the novice Unix user. For example, on a typical non-Unix system, the user might type the following command in a directory containing no files. Notice how the system responds by informing the user that no files were found:

```
$DIR
DIRECTORY: NO FILES FOUND
$
```

Contrast the above response with that of the Unix *ls* command. When it doesn't find any files in a directory, it simply returns to the command prompt:

```
sh> ls
sh>
```

Many people familiar with non-Unix systems often criticize Unix for failing to inform the user that the directory is empty. Unix advocates, on the other hand, argue that Unix has indeed informed the user that no files were found with the refusal of the *ls* command to print any file names. The lack of file names is proof itself that the directory is empty. It's like saying that it's dark in a room instead of saying that there are no lights on. A subtle difference, yes, but an important one.

Are there any advantages to having commands that operate silently when no data is present? For one thing, your screen contains only meaningful data instead of being cluttered with commentary that transmits little useful information. It is easier to find trickles of data if they are not surrounded by an ocean of detail.

Although this keeps things simple, there is a more technical reason. As we discussed earlier, most Unix commands act as filters that are often combined using the Unix pipe mechanism. For example:

```
ls -l | awk '{print $4}' | sort
```

The *-l* parameter instructs *ls* to produce a longer, comprehensive file listing. The pipe symbol '|' connects the *ls* command's output to the *awk* command's input. The *'{print $4}'* part directs *awk* to print only the fourth field of each line of text produced by *ls* and discard the rest. This field is passed to the *sort* command, which sorts each field in alphabetical order.

In the typical scenario, such as when the directory contains several files, everything works as described above. But what happens when the directory is empty? Since *ls* produces no output, the pipeline breaks immediately and no further processing by *awk* and *sort* occurs. If, however, *ls* produced "DIRECTORY: NO FILES FOUND" on its output to the pipeline, this would result in a strange "FOUND" message appearing as the final output from the *sort* command, since "FOUND" is the fourth field in the message. *Ls* may not seem very user friendly because it doesn't warn explicitly of an empty directory, but its design both informs the user that the directory is empty and makes it possible for *ls* to be used in pipelines.

One Unix system administrator pointed out that system logs are a real lifesaver for him. Without the extra output, he says, he would be unable to solve some of the configuration problems he has seen. In cases where the extra output is necessary for debugging purposes, it is easy enough to redirect just the error information to a log file for later perusal.

Under Unix it is important that you say what you mean—nothing more, nothing less.

7.6   **Think parallel**

There is an old joke in the computer world that goes something like this: If one woman can have a baby in nine months, does that mean that nine women can have a baby in one month? The obvious implication here is that certain tasks must be performed serially due to nature. No attempts to make the process run in parallel will make the result appear any faster.

Motherhood aside, there are many processes in the world today that can be and are done in parallel. Construction work crews, television production teams, and professional basketball teams are all examples of entities that must operate in parallel. To meet their goals, they function as a collection of serial operatives taking place simultaneously, each member of which performs a part of the total task. They meet at certain points to ensure their progress toward their goal, not unlike the way semaphores and other interprocess mechanisms used in computer applications keep themselves synchronized.

In a Unix sense, thinking parallel usually means that you try to keep the central processing unit busy. Most of today's CPUs far outdistance the ability of mass storage devices such as hard drives, floppy disks, and even memory chips to keep up with them. To get the most out of a system, you must keep the processor busy so that it doesn't have to wait for the peripherals to catch up.

The Unix approach is to run multiple processes simultaneously, with each process scheduled to do part of the overall task. That way when any process becomes blocked while waiting for the peripheral devices, several other processes can still function. This results in enormous efficiencies. Consequently, Unix often outperforms other operating systems on the same hardware platform in terms of the total work being done.

Parallelism also greatly affects how users perceive your application. Unix users have long enjoyed "net news," a large collection of articles (files) distributed throughout the world via the Internet network and the Unix-to-Unix copy program *uucp*. The files cover an incredibly broad range of topics, and thousands of new files appear daily. Net news and other similar forums are the ultimate electronic town meetings.

One problem with net news is that some news groups, as they are called, will often occupy directories on a system containing thousands of files. Such directories are slow and cumbersome to open to obtain a list of files and their headers. Software in the past often required several minutes to open a single large news directory. This frustrated users immensely. It made it extremely difficult when one wanted to hop quickly from news group to news group.

Along came a program written by Larry Wall called *rn*. It read news group directories the same as any other program with one small catch: It obtained directory listings "in the background" while the user was reading messages. It quietly did this action unbeknownst to the user. The key difference is that when the user decided he or she would like to switch to a different news group, *rn* had likely already "prefetched" its contents so it could immediately display them. It's like calling ahead for pizza so it will be ready when you get there.

While thinking in parallel has obvious advantages for the *rn* user interface, it can have equally dramatic effects in other kinds of software as well. For example, Unix allows a command to be run in the background by appending "&" to the command line. Commands invoked this way start a process running in parallel to the command interpreter or shell. It is possible to run several tasks simultaneously this way. This improves efficiency by keeping the CPU busy most of the time instead of idling while waiting for peripherals to complete their I/O requests.

A final point to keep in mind about thinking in parallel is this: No matter how fast a machine may be, you can always create a faster one by stringing several of them together. As the prices of CPU chips continue to plummet, it will become more desirable in the future to run systems having hundreds, thousands, or even millions of processors. By devoting a small unifunctional program to each processor, it will be possible to accomplish tasks that most people consider impossible today. Unix has already established itself as a leader in such environments. Linux is expected to dominate there as well.

7.7   The sum of the parts is greater than the whole

The venerable claw hammer has been a part of the carpenter's trade for about as long as we have had nails. Used for both driving nails and pulling them, it combines two utility functions on a single wooden handle. Some claw hammers may have improved handles or tempered steel claws, but the basic idea is still the same. The idea has stood the test of time.

Or has it?

Most professional carpenters still use claw hammers today, but the hammer's turf is being challenged by new technologies. The hammer is no longer the best tool for the job, only a convenient substitute. For instance, nail guns have outpaced its ability to drive nails. They do the job much faster with greater accuracy. Nail guns enable workers to construct houses in a fraction of the time needed in the past. The hammer's claw end, however, remains secure. It appears that there is little that high tech can do for the universal wrecking bar.

Some people's software resembles the hammer. It provides a convenient conglomeration of functions that mate well to complete a task. The problem is, many integrated applications like these exist as large, monolithic programs. Sure, they get the job done, but they overwhelm the user—and the system—by incorporating features that may never be understood, let alone used, by the average user.

The Unix approach to building integrated applications is to construct them out of a collection of small components. This way you load and use only the functions you need. You also retain the flexibility to modify selected portions of the application without requiring the replacement of the entire application. Consider Figure 7.1:

Figure 7.1

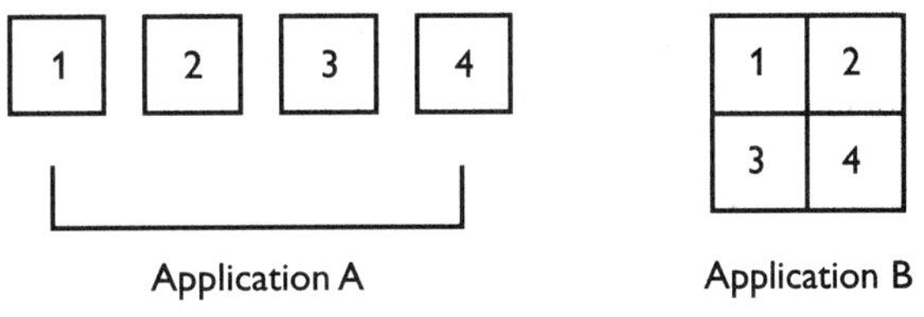

Application A   Application B

When fast-track Unix and Linux software developers design an application program, they strive for the solution that will give them the biggest bang for their buck, so to speak. This means eliminating those functions that few people use and that are costly to implement. They ruthlessly cut such functions from the product requirements, often with the attitude of if someone needs this capability badly enough, they can do it themselves.

Obviously, there are some situations, such as heart transplants, where a 90-percent solution won't suffice. These are rare in the computer world, though. Remember that most software is a compromise in that it is never finished, only released. If, by definition, software can never be finished, one can never develop software that offers a 100-percent implementation. By recognizing the 90-percent solution as a reasonable measure of completeness, it becomes easy to write applications that appeal to most of the user population.

That is part of the reason for Unix's success. While it avoids trying to be everything to everyone, it meets the needs of most. The rest can write their own operating systems.

7.9   Worse is better

Anyone who has ever been in the military knows that there is the right way, the wrong way, and the military way.

The "right way" is the way that I know is right, you know is right, and every normal person knows is right. It is what we consider correct—in every aspect. It is undeniably proper. The shoe fits. It works.

The "wrong way" stands as the inverse of the right way. Blatantly incorrect, it is wrong, dead wrong, no matter who looks at it. Your mother and father know it's wrong, your kid brother agrees, and your broker guarantees it.

The most enigmatic, the "military way" is by far the most interesting of the three. While the right way and the wrong way coexist in an inverse relationship, the military way enshrouds itself in a cloud that is neither black nor white. It is the way in which those things that ought to work mysteriously fail, and—better yet—those things that should fail miserably unwittingly achieve unprecedented success.

The "Unix way" is akin to the military way. If you listen to the purists, Unix should have withered and died 20 years ago. Yet, here it is in its entire parasitic splendor, feeding off the criticisms leveled at it by its critics and growing stronger every day.

Ingrained within the Unix way is the paradoxical notion that "worse is better." Many claim that Unix is not nearly as good as such-and-such system because its user interface is terrible or that Unix is too simple to be considered a serious operating system. Linux, too, once received its share of criticism because it lacked a reasonable GUI, it was difficult to install, and it lacked a viable office application software package.

Yet, if Unix is worse than most other systems in so many ways, then it only proves that "worse" has a better chance of survival than that which is either "right" or "wrong." For Unix and Linux have shown a remarkable ability to persist in a world where new technologies continually render existing technologies obsolete.

There exists a school of thought in the computer world that says that all proper designs should have four characteristics: simplicity, correctness, consistency, and completeness. Designs should be simple, correct (bug-free) in all observable aspects, consistent throughout, and complete in that they must cover all cases one can reasonably expect.

Most Unix programmers will agree that applications and systems should be simple, correct, consistent, and complete. The key is how they prioritize those characteristics. Although the proper system designer strives for completeness at the expense of simplicity, Unix developers elevate simplicity to the primary priority. So the proper system designer levels criticism at Unix, not so much because it is improper, but because its priorities are reversed. In that sense, it is worse than the proper system.

Unix aficionados, on the other hand, point to the survival characteristics of worse and say that worse is better. Look at the VHS videotape format, they say. VHS tapes are big and "clunky" compared to Sony's Beta tapes. They do not record nearly as well. They are hardly a match for optical disks. Yet, VHS tapes clearly dominated the home-video market compared with the Beta format. Today, of course, DVDs are replacing VHS tapes, as they are even cheaper.

Similarly, the user interface on the Windows PCs comes nowhere near the practically flawless user interface on the Apple machines. Still, PCs are on more desks than Apple machines, even if PCs are much worse than Macintoshes from a user perspective.

One reason for the success of Unix is that it has always been regarded as an operating system that is worse than others in many respects. It was never used for any so-called serious work, as such tasks were usually left to industrial-strength commercial operating systems. Unix typically occupied the lower echelon of hardware configurations instead. It found a home on the minicomputer, a machine that lacked the brute force of a large mainframe, but was powerful enough for more mundane work. Since minicomputers were typically used for less important tasks, it didn't make sense for hardware vendors to invest lots of money in minicomputer operating systems, at least as far as the scientific community was concerned. This tendency was further exaggerated when workstations came along. It became cheaper to simply port an existing system obtained for the cost of the media.

Today it isn't very difficult to find commercial versions of applications that are better than the free software available on Linux. Most free software lacks the features and polish of good commercial packages. Yet the growth of the free software applications easily outstrips that of commercial packages.

Some vendors and industry consortiums today are working to make Linux better. In doing so, they hope that it will lose its worse-is-better character and finally will be taken seriously. This could a fatal mistake. For if Linux is made into something that is truly better in all respects, then it runs the risk of extinction. In becoming "better," it will need to favor completeness at the expense of simplicity. Once that happens, a new operating system will likely emerge that embodies the tenets of the Unix philosophy better than the system Linux may have evolved into.

7.10   Think hierarchically

Several years ago it became necessary for the first time to explain to my daughter how to organize files in a directory hierarchy. Before then, she had only a rudimentary knowledge of file system layouts. She understood that there was a directory on the family computer's hard disk with her name on it. If she clicked the mouse pointer on the correct icons in the GUI, she could obtain a list of those files she considered her own.

Alas, youth has more time than experience. As a nine-year-old, she had enough free time to create a collection of drawings so large that the file listings would scroll off the screen. In the interest of making her directory more manageable for her, I showed her the benefits of creating multiple subdirectories for her picture files. It didn't take long before she realized that she could also create directories within directories, so she could organize her drawings in neatly organized electronic folders nestled five levels deep.

She had learned to think hierarchically.

It's a simple idea, but like so much else in Unix, it has profound significance. While it seems obvious to many today that file systems should be laid out hierarchically, this wasn't always so. Early operating systems often placed system-related files in one directory and the users' files in directories all at the same level in the directory tree. People couldn't see the benefits of hierarchical thinking in those days.

Most modern operating systems organize files and directories in hierarchies, and Unix is no exception. Unix differs slightly from other systems, however, in the syntax one uses to reference files nested deeply within multiple directory levels. Unix is conveniently consistent in using the "/" character to separate the components of a file's path name. Thus:

```
/usr/a/users/gancarz/.profile
```

represents the file ".profile" in the directory "gancarz." The directory "gancarz" is found within the directory "users," and so on up to the directory "/", which is the "root" directory.[2] The Unix file system hierarchy is essentially an upside-down tree, with the root directory sitting atop successive branches (directories) and leaf nodes (files).

Unix organizes other components hierarchically, too. For example, tasks in Unix, known as processes, occupy a tree structure. Process number 1, the *init* process, serves as the root of the tree. All other processes—including user sessions—are the offspring of *init* or its child processes. A process spawns a child process by creating a copy of itself and marking itself as the parent process of the child. Just as in real life, the child process inherits the attributes of its parent.

Another example of the hierarchical approach in Unix is the X Window System's user interface library. It uses a resource manager that allows user

---

2.   Microsoft Windows organizes files and folders hierarchically as well. However, users must always be aware of the physical drive or partition (e.g., the C: drive). The root directory on Unix, however, represents the top of a tree that includes all drives on the system as opposed to having separate root directories for each physical drive. Unix users need not be concerned about the (often complex) physical drive and partition layouts on their systems. Under Unix, it's all one big tree.

interface objects, such as buttons and menus, to inherit attributes from other user interface objects hierarchically. This powerful idea makes it possible for users to customize fonts, colors, and other attributes in several components of an application.

Apart from the practical uses within Unix, there is also a philosophical reason for hierarchical thinking. No one can deny that most of nature is ordered hierarchically as well. To use an old cliché, the mighty oak that grows from a small acorn eventually will produce acorns of its own. Those acorns will in turn produce more oak trees. This cycle has been repeating itself since the dawn of time. Similarly, in human nature, parents beget children that in turn grow up to beget children of their own. The idea of a family tree has its roots, so to speak, in the trees of the forest. Since the hierarchical organization of Unix mirrors nature, it's a very good sign that it's probably a good approach.

In this chapter we have explored 10 lesser tenets of the Unix philosophy. It is not expected that all members of the Unix or Linux communities at large will agree with everything discussed here. That is of little concern. The Unix community, like the rest of the free world, allows for a great degree of individual expression and occasional disagreement.

Some of these ideas can also be found in other operating systems. Whether Unix is the originator or the recipient of these tenets is unclear. Nevertheless, many Unix users and programmers follow them, knowingly or otherwise. The same holds true for the Linux community.

8

Making Unix Do One Thing Well

Most of what we've covered thus far has been abstract. Although we have seen that there are practical reasons behind every tenet of the Unix philosophy, some of you may still believe that they wouldn't work in the real world. "Small is beautiful" is fine, but what about the big jobs? Is it really possible to build a complete application from a collection of small programs? Can a program without a CUI serve a useful purpose? These are fair questions, to be sure. You will find the answers to them and more in this chapter.

We're going to look at MH, a mail-handling application developed by the RAND Corporation. It consists of a series of programs that when combined give the user an enormous ability to manipulate email messages. A complex application, it shows that not only is it possible to build large applications from smaller components, but also that such designs are actually preferable.

If a program is valuable, it will be ported from one platform to the next. Such is the case with MH. The original ideas remain the same, but newer versions have come along through the years that enhance the original. In today's Linux distributions, New MH (NMH) has largely superceded MH. NMH incorporates all of the major features of MH and—most importantly—adheres to the original philosophy of MH. For the purpose of this discussion, we will be covering the ideas behind MH, recognizing that they apply equally well to NMH.

Before Web-based email came along, two programs—/bin/mail and Berkeley Mail—had been used almost exclusively for many years to process email under Unix. Although Berkeley Mail was used heavily, both programs are poor examples of applications with respect to the Unix philosophy. Both employ CUIs, have limited capabilities as filters, and, in the case of Berkeley Mail, can hardly be considered small programs. Neither focuses on doing one thing well, opting instead to incorporate a range of mail-related functions within a single user interface.

MH provides capabilities equivalent to those in both /bin/mail and Berkeley Mail. It is a collection of small programs, each of which performs a function found in the other two mailers. MH also provides other small programs that perform actions not available with the other two, almost as if to underscore the ease with which one can incorporate new functions in an application modeled under the Unix philosophy.

The following is a partial list of the commands contained within MH:

ali	List mail aliases
anno	Annotate message
burst	Explode digests into messages
comp	Compose a message
dist	Redistribute a message to additional addresses
folder	Set/list current folder/message
folders	List all folders
forw	Forward messages
inc	Incorporate new mail
mark	Mark messages
mhl	Produce formatted listing of MH messages
mhmail	Send or read mail
mhook	MH receive-mail hooks
mhpath	Print full pathnames of MH messages and folders
msgchk	Check for messages
msh	MH shell (and BBoard reader)
next	Show the next message
packf	Compress a folder into a single file
pick	Select messages by content
prev	Show the previous message
prompter	Prompting editor front end
rcvstore	Incorporate new mail asynchronously
refile	File messages in other folders
repl	Reply to a message
rmf	Remove folder
rmm	Remove messages
scan	Produce a one-line-per-message scan listing
send	Send a message
show	Show (list) messages
sortm	Sort messages
vmh	Visual front end to MH

whatnow	Prompting front end for send
whom	Report to whom a message should go

MH uses a collection of folders to organize a user's mail. It stores each mail message as a separate file within a folder. The inbox folder has a special purpose: The contents of the user's system mailbox are first placed in the inbox by the *inc* command. Once mail has been moved to the inbox, it can then be selected and acted upon by the rest of the MH commands without having to specify a folder.

As you can see from the list, MH provides all of the capabilities you would expect from a comprehensive email application. The *scan* command displays the sender, date, and subject line of a range of messages in the current folder. The commands *show, next,* and *prev* show the contents of selected mail messages, the next message in the current folder, or the previous message in the folder, respectively. *Comp* and *repl* allow you to create a new mail message or reply to an existing one.

The major difference between MH and the other Unix mailers is that you can invoke any of the mail-handling functions from the shell-prompt level. This gives MH tremendous flexibility. Since each function is a command unto itself, you can call functions like any other command under Unix.

The commands can be used within shell scripts and as filters. The output of *scan*, for example, can be "piped" into the Unix *grep* text-search command to locate mail from a specific sender quickly. If the folder contains so many messages that *scan*'s output scrolls off the screen, the output can be piped into the Unix *more* command to allow the user to view the list a page at a time. If the user wanted to look at a listing of only the last five messages, *scan | tail -5* does the trick.[1]

The point here is that the user is not limited to the functional capabilities built into MH by the original programmer. One need only combine MH commands with other Unix commands to create new and useful functions. This requires no new programming. The user mixes and matches the commands as desired. If the desired capability doesn't exist, it can be created

---

1.   These are not the only ways to perform these functions. As in the rest of Unix, many paths lead to the same conclusion. The examples shown were chosen to illustrate the flexibility of a Unix-style architecture.

immediately with very little effort. Many new functions are developed on the fly on the user's command line using this simple yet powerful architecture.

A valid question people sometimes raise about MH is, how do you remember which commands are available? Those who are familiar with the Berkeley Mail command, for example, know that they can always type "?" to get a list of available commands. MH really shines in this area. Since it doesn't use a CUI, you can refer to the on-line Unix manual pages at any time. These manual pages are considerably more thorough than the short list of commands provided by Mail. MH's operation is therefore much better documented as there is typically a full page of documentation (or more!) per individual command.

What about the user who prefers a CUI? MH provides one with the *msh* command for those users who enjoy being prompted for the next action to take. Obviously, though, users are not locked into using *msh* if they choose not to. They are free to write their own user interface that works as a layer on top of the MH command set. For example, *xmh* is a user interface to MH that runs as a client under the X Window System. Buttons and menu items in the *xmh* application simply call underlying MH commands as appropriate. The *xmh* user interface presents a seamless interface to the user, however. It appears as if it were written as an application that performs the mail-handing functions directly.

MH offers us an excellent example of a specific way to build a complex application under Unix. Figure 8.1 illustrates the more general case.

The Small Programs Layer consists of a set of Unix commands or shell scripts, each of which carries out one function of the application. As new capabilities are needed, it is an easy matter to create other small programs to provide the desired functions. On the other hand, if a more limited application is wanted, nothing need be done. The Application Layer simply refrains from calling those programs that are unnecessary.

The Application Layer determines the functions that are essential to the user. The functions themselves are carried out by the Small Programs Layer. It

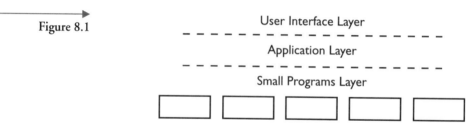

Figure 8.1

encapsulates the business rules and provides boundaries around the application. The Application Layer operates primarily as a liaison between the Small Programs Layer and the User Interface Layer. By unifying elements of the Small Programs Layer in a single environment, it helps establish the relationship among the small programs and provides the framework that ties them together. In other words, it is the integration layer.

The User Interface Layer is the part that the user sees on the screen when the application is invoked. It is highly malleable in that a variety of user interface styles can be used depending on the desired presentation. Three styles of user interfaces are most common in the Unix environment: the command-driven user interface, where parameters are passed to the command from the command line; the scrolling menu type, a kind of CUI where parameters are collected from a series of interactive dialogs with the user; and the GUI, typically found on a PC with graphical capabilities such as those found under the X Window System.

A well-constructed Application Layer allows the user to choose from a variety of user interface styles, implying that the User Interface Layer should almost never be "hardwired." The user should be free to choose whatever user interface suits the particular circumstances. Thus, a user can take advantage of the superior power afforded by a GUI for occasional usage, yet still choose to use, say, a scrolling menu interface when performance is important. MH and its companion *xmh* provide an example of an application that incorporates this kind of flexibility.

8.1   The Unix philosophy: Putting it all together

In the previous chapter we saw how the whole is often greater than the sum of its parts. This is especially true of the Unix philosophy itself: Each of its tenets hardly has the strength to stand on its own. Storing data in flat text files doesn't buy much unless you have the tools to manipulate it. The goal of portability over efficiency seems shallow without shell scripts and the C language to accomplish it. Writing a collection of small programs makes little sense if they cannot be used as filters.

The Unix philosophy is like a giant water slide at an amusement park. You cannot decide part way into the ride that you'd like to skip a few curves—you'll only wind up on the ground bruised and bleeding. As many have discovered the hard way, the Unix philosophy doesn't work if you employ it piecemeal.

Embraced together, however, the tenets of the Unix philosophy take on a broader, more powerful dimension. They interoperate and reinforce one another. Any criticism leveled at a lone tenet can be met by a response from another tenet. The old adage, "united we stand, divided we fall" rings true here.

Let's visit the Unix philosophy once more. This time, though, we will focus on the relationships among the tenets, the goal being to expose the synergy you get by using them together.

Small programs have definite advantages. They are easier to understand because people have less difficulty dealing with a small something than a large something. Their being easier to understand also means that they are easier to maintain. Therefore, they are more cost effective in the end. They also use fewer system resources. This enables them to be loaded, run, and then released quickly, yielding greater efficiency, an attribute that must often be sacrificed for the sake of greater portability. Finally, small programs combine easily with other tools. By themselves, they do little. In concert with a suite of other small programs, they enable programmers and—most importantly—users to create new applications rapidly.

Small programs should remain focused (i.e., they should do one thing well). It is more important to solve one problem than a slew of them in a single program. By dividing large complex problems into smaller ones, it becomes possible to conquer them a bit at a time. Programs that do one thing well can be reused in other applications with much less difficulty. Their abilities are well defined and not clouded by useless "cruft" that can obscure a program's functional definition.

Small programs that do one thing well avoid becoming large complex monoliths. Such monoliths often contain "spaghetti code" and are difficult to join with other applications. Small programs acknowledge that there is a tomorrow where today's functional capabilities will appear incomplete or, worse, obsolete. Whereas monolithic programs cover all known circumstances, small programs freely admit that software evolves. Software is never finished; it is only released.

Because the world's software is in a constant state of evolution, everyone is on a learning curve. No one can predict with absolute certainty the directions that the software world will take tomorrow. The best that one can do is build software that meets the needs of today with the built-in assumption that it will change in the future. Therefore, instead of spending weeks or months writing design specifications, developers should document an overview of the direction they plan to take and then get on with it.

Building a prototype early is an important step. It helps the designer get an application into the hands of others early so that progress toward the Third System begins sooner instead of later. Prototypes accelerate the rate at which you move into the future. They encourage you to make changes at first when things are still fluid instead of waiting until everything is cast in stone. They show you what will work and—most importantly—what won't.

Building prototypes is much easier if you construct them gradually using small programs that do one thing well. This allows you to add functions as you go along with minimal effort.

Remember that software isn't really built, however. It's grown. As software grows, it will undoubtedly become more valuable as it is ported to new hardware platforms. When new architectures come along, software that is portable can take advantage of them quickly. Therefore, when constructing prototypes, choose portability over efficiency. That which is portable survives. All else quickly becomes obsolete.

Portable data goes hand in hand with portable applications. Store data in flat text files whenever possible. Again, we cannot predict the future, so you cannot know all the places your data might eventually go. Do not be concerned that portable data is not very efficient. New hardware platforms just around the bend will move your data around considerably faster than even the fastest machine can today. Remember, too, that the use of portable data also simplifies the process of getting to the Third System, because the data is readable by humans at all stages of the process.

Portable software finds its way onto hardware platforms that you never dreamed of when you wrote it. In a sense, by writing portable software, you make a contribution to the wealth of software that has been written since the dawn of computing. Bear in mind that for whatever software you give to the world, you are also entitled to receive software as well. As your software travels, it will enhance the abilities of users to carry out their tasks.

The effects of nearly everything you do are compounded. Similarly, there are other programmers whose work is compounding. For you to take advantage of that leverage, shun the NIH syndrome entirely. Create new applications, but do not waste time rewriting what someone else has already written for you. The software that exists in the world today represents a great store of wealth. As you sow seeds in that realm, be sure to harvest that which is ripe for the taking—legally, of course.

To greater enhance software leverage in both directions, employ scripts and other higher-level abstractions whenever possible. They take advantage of the work that others have done for you. Scripts help compound the effects of their work on the world, while enabling you to do more with less effort.

Scripts can be constructed much more easily if you have a collection of small programs to work with. Those programs won't be much good, though, if they require a user to type into them directly. Therefore, avoid CUIs. Instead, think of all programs as filters. Programs do not create data. They only modify it. Make it easy for your programs to be used elsewhere.

Synergy. It's all about synergy.

Is that all? Well, yeah. Most Unix and Linux programs, by themselves, are nothing to write home about. You can always find a better word-processing program or a fancier e-mail program or a prettier view of a directory folder than you'll find on a Unix system. (However, some Linux GUI applications are fairly impressive in their own right.) Try to do something with text that the monolithic word processor wasn't designed to do,[2] however, and you'll find that Unix is very, very capable.

Proponents of other operating systems claim that a particular operating system can do this or that better than Unix. That may be true in some instances. Even then, Unix (and Linux, as it matures) will likely be able to provide 90 percent of the solution in a fraction of the time it would take to write a new application. Furthermore, Unix can provide this 90-percent solution in virtually all cases, even in those situations where it seemingly would not be able to do so.

But hold on. We're getting ahead of ourselves here. If you want to learn how the Unix philosophy compares with other operating system philosophies, it's time to proceed to the next chapter.

---

2.   If you've ever tried to modify a text string in a thousand documents according to dynamically changing business rules, then you understand one limitation of word processors. That takes a really good filter program. On the other hand, if you're trying to create the first version of a document, then a word processor makes a fine tool.

9

Unix and Other Operating System Philosophies

At this juncture, it is appropriate to engage in a short discussion of the philosophies of a few other operating systems besides Unix. We're not going to delve deeply into this area, as we do not intend to embark upon a treatise on comparative operating system philosophies. But a brief foray into several other "religions" of the software world should prove enlightening, if only to illuminate why the Unix approach is such a radical departure from other software design methodologies.

We will look at the design philosophies of three historical operating systems in this chapter. Each had achieved success in its respective niche. Each had developed a following of loyal devotees. Each shares some commonality with Unix and Linux, and each bears some characteristics that set it apart, sometimes in striking ways.

For a variety of reasons, not the least of which was limited hardware capacity, these operating systems were written for specific hardware platforms. Users needed strong justification to shell out several thousand to several million dollars for systems that were relatively inflexible. You did not have thousands of applications available at discount retailers and flea markets. Personal computers were not cheap and plentiful. Few people had old computers collecting dust on the tops of piles of unused household goods in their basements.

Newer, faster hardware eventually came along, causing these OSs to fall into disuse. Without the portability of Unix, they could not keep up as hardware designers produced machines with increasing amounts of storage, specialized peripherals, and advanced graphics capabilities. The one exception here is Microsoft's Disk Operating System (MS-DOS). MS-DOS is not a portable operating system, however. It was ported to progressively more powerful machines, but they were all of essentially the same architecture. In more recent versions of Windows, Microsoft has all but eliminated MS-DOS altogether in favor of the Windows API and GUI.

Although the operating systems discussed here have themselves largely faded into obscurity, their design philosophies still exist today in one form or another. For example, while production of the Atari Home Computer ceased long ago, the human engineering concepts found in its operating system continue to be implemented and refined in today's hottest game machines.

If I manage to misinterpret the original intent of the operating system designers, I offer my apologies. As you might suspect, documented operating system philosophies are hard to come by. I can only hope that I have caught the essence of the designers' goals in some fashion. For our purposes, though, absolute accuracy is less important than the general thread of the design methodology in a holistic sense. In that respect, the following discussions should serve us well.

9.1   The Atari Home Computer: Human engineering as art

The Atari 800 and its less expensive sibling, the Atari 400, garnered a respectable share of the home-computer market in the early 1980s. Primarily targeted as a machine for game enthusiasts, its claim to fame was its advanced graphics and sound capabilities. Star Raiders, a Star Trek simulation incorporating stars and photon torpedoes whizzing by in 3-D hyperspace, propelled it to a strong position in the home market until it was overtaken by the popular IBM PC and the bargain-priced Commodore 64. Today its "player-missile" graphics (sprites) and display list processor are considered primitive.

The designers of Unix and the Atari Home Computer's operating system had a common goal in that they both wanted to build a system for playing games—namely, Space Travel on Unix and games in general on the Atari. (Pac-Man?) That may be one reason why they were successful. People will often work long and hard on something that brings them pleasure. Today, many developers write software for Linux for the sheer fun of it. To them, this is entertainment, geek-style. Beyond a need for survival and social order, people have a built-in need to be entertained. It may seem strange to those outside of the computer world, but many Linux geeks find software development to be a great pastime.

Chris Crawford, a member of Atari's staff at the time, heavily influenced the design of the Atari Home Computer's operating system. His application software (games, really) set the standard by which all later software for the machine was to be judged. Crawford documented much of his design philosophy in Appendix B of *De Re Atari: A Guide to Effective Programming*. While the section's main focus is human engineering, it also sheds much light on Crawford's general approach to computing.

Crawford views the computer as an intelligent being lacking outward physical traits. Its thought processes are "direct, analytical, and specific." He contrasts these with the thought patterns of human beings, which are "associative, integrated, and diffuse." The differences in these thought processes create a communication barrier between these human beings and this smaller intelligence, or homunculus, as he calls it. The goal of the programmer, he believes, is not so much to make the homunculus more powerful as it is to break down the communication barrier between the homunculus and the person interacting with it.

This is where Crawford's approach and the Unix philosophy part company. For while Crawford emphasizes that the most important thing a piece of software can do is to communicate with a human being, a Unix program's highest priority is to communicate with another program. That the Unix program must eventually interact with a human being is secondary.

In their approach to user interface design, the Atari Home Computer and the Unix operating system are galaxies apart. Most software for the Atari machine strives for "closure," or the narrowing of options. According to Crawford,

> The ideal program is like a tunnel bored through solid rock. There is but one path, the path leading to success. The user has no options but to succeed.[1]

To create the optimum Atari Home Computer program you must limit choices. The user should be given only one way to perform a task, and that way should be obvious. There must be little opportunity for error, even if it means limiting choices. Using Crawford's line of thinking, the flexibility and adaptability found in the Unix and Linux worlds can only lead to chaos.

Modern game machines implement the same philosophy as the software found on the Atari Home Computer. They limit choices. They make it nearly impossible for kids to make a wrong selection. They ensure that the gamer will usually have a pleasurable, if somewhat limited, experience with the computer.

Limiting choices within a computer system can be challenging. For while users are constantly seeking out the latest whiz-bang thrill, they want to do so within the confines of a constrained world. They want to be adventurous, but not too adventurous. They must be able to walk away from the ride afterwards so they can ride again.

The Atari approach suggests that if the average person is given a gun, he is likely to shoot himself in the foot. By contrast, the Unix system effectively hands the uninitiated user an assault rifle, plugs in 20 rounds, and points it

---

1.   *De Re Atari: A Guide to Effective Programming,* ©1982 Atari, Inc.

at his foot. A person with his foot shot off doesn't walk away from the ride very easily.

As you might expect, the Unix way can wreak havoc. Choices abound in the Unix environment, and limitations are few. There usually exist at least a dozen ways to perform any task. This comparative abundance of freedom often pushes new users' patience to the edge, as ill-chosen commands plunder their data and leave them wondering how to salvage it. But eventually most Unix power users find that understanding replaces chaos, and flexibility and adaptability find favor over artificial limitations. For those who have no interest in becoming Unix power users, the various Linux distributions come with GUIs that hide most of the complexity underneath the covers.

Mainstream computer users have grown quite comfortable over time with a progressively narrower set of choices. At one point, there were several office application suites in common usage on PCs, each offering its particular set of features and strengths. Today Microsoft Office clearly dominates this space. Many business offices refuse to use anything else. Some say this simplifies things in that everyone can share documents more easily if the same application suite produces them all. The downside is that this limits creativity. If the document format were made a public standard, then new and interesting applications would come along that would adhere to the standard and offer added value beyond that provided by a single vendor. As good as Microsoft Office is—it is a feature-rich application suite—one must believe that Microsoft doesn't hold the world's entire cache of creativity captive in Redmond.

One has only to look at the cable-television market to realize that the number of choices that consumers are faced with is increasing, not decreasing. About 40 years ago, back at the tail end of the Industrial Age, you had a choice of three television networks in America. Today the typical digital cable system offers hundreds of channels. And that number will only increase as the population grows and its viewing interests become more diverse.

In the Information Age, the number of choices increases dramatically. The "tunnel through solid rock" becomes a series of passageways each arriving at an end point tailored for a particular user. Like the users of the Atari Home Computer, new or occasional computer users require user interfaces that limit choices, making it difficult to fail. Intermediate users want more features and options but not at the expense of making the simple tasks too difficult. No one wants to drink from a fire hose directly. The "power users" want access to all that the system offers without the impediments of user interfaces that hide their options.

This is where Linux steps in. With GUIs like KDE and other environments, it offers multiple entry points for novice users. As these environments improve, Microsoft Windows and other GUI-based OSs will lose ground as the only game in town for new users, slowly succumbing to an onslaught of desktops, some of which may be even easier to use. Power users under Linux find that its distinctly open architecture and interfaces leave room for plenty of flexibility in ways that closed architectures cannot.

Now, if we could just get Chris Crawford to write a really cool version of Star Raiders for Linux.

9.2   MS-DOS: Over seventy million users can't be wrong

Before the advent of Microsoft's Windows NT and successive Windows generations, MS-DOS, was the operating system under the covers of the then current personal computers. At one point, over seventy million people used MS-DOS daily. If the number of users running your operating system solely determines your criterion for success, then MS-DOS can easily claim to be the most successful non-Windows operating system in history.[2]

The "herd mentality" largely accounts for the overwhelming success of MS-DOS in America. While small cars opened America's wallet and bank accounts in the early 1980s, small computers captured the hearts and minds of millions of people who needed to store and manage information on a personal level (i.e., just about everybody). When IBM built a capable machine and used its marketing muscle to hype it to a public ripe for a "personal computer," the herd quickly adopted it. What better company to fuel such a revolution than the General Motors of the business-machine industry?

So MS-DOS gained tremendous acceptance, not because it represented a giant step forward in the design of operating systems, but because it ran on a system considered a safe bet by the herd. As the saying goes, no one was ever fired for buying IBM. Combine this with Microsoft's aggressive marketing of

---

2.   Another measure for success is the number of *nonhuman* users of a program has. The more *other programs* execute a program, the better the program is. See Chapter 10.

MS-DOS to IBM PC "clone" manufacturers, and you had a formula for a phenomenon that the herd would consider a safe bet.

Over time, this phenomenon began to take on a life of its own. As more people bought MS-DOS machines, software application vendors began to recognize MS-DOS as the platform of choice. Additional MS-DOS applications became available as a result, making MS-DOS more attractive to more people.

This cycle continues today in a similar way with Linux, the new kid on the Unix block. The more applications become available under Linux, the more it becomes the operating system of choice.

So what is the philosophy behind MS-DOS? First, simplicity is paramount. If you're going to design an operating system for the herd, then you want it to be easy for most of the herd's members to use. Hence, MS-DOS has a concise, limited command language. There is little latitude for the sophisticated user. On the other hand, the limitations of the command set are offset by an often verbose set of help and error messages. For example, the following notice is typical under MS-DOS:

WARNING! ALL DATA ON NON-REMOVABLE DISK DRIVE
C: WILL BE LOST...PROCEED WITH FORMAT (Y/N)?

Second, by limiting user input and increasing system output, the MS-DOS designers have made the user more passenger than driver. This helps preserve the illusion that the user is seated at the console of a huge mainframe machine. Unfortunately, this defeats the purpose of using a personal computer.

Unix has, by comparison, a fairly potent command language, so much so that even experienced users sometimes fail to take full advantage of its power. Whereas the command language may be nearly unlimited, though, its error message set is painfully concise. "Do you know what you're doing?" is about as strong a warning message as you'll get from *mkfs*, a potentially destructive Unix utility used to initialize new file systems.

Perhaps the most surprising aspect of the MS-DOS environment is that it incorporates some Unix concepts already. For example, MS-DOS provides a "pipe" feature much like the Unix pipe mechanism, as well as a tree-like directory structure. MS-DOS also contains the *MORE* command, which functions much like the *more* command found in Unix implementations. This suggests that there may have been some persons familiar with Unix involved in the early design stages of MS-DOS.

The Unix pipe mechanism allows the output from one command to be fed directly into another command's input without the use of temporary files. A quick example is

```
find / | grep part
```

This command is really two commands—*find* and *grep*. The *find* command outputs a list of the names of all files on the system. The *grep* command selects only those file names containing the string "part." The pipe symbol "|" is the "pipeline" that allows the data to pass from the output of *find* to the input of *grep*.

Both the *find* and *grep* commands are invoked simultaneously in a style of computing known as "multitasking." As data becomes available on the output of *find*, it is passed directly to *grep*.

MS-DOS pipes differ from Unix pipes, however, in that MS-DOS doesn't provide true multitasking capability. Only one command runs at a time, regardless of how commands are entered on the command line.

In the early 1990s, it looked as though follow-on versions of MS-DOS might contain additional Unix-like features. For example, MS-DOS Version 6 added the ability to support multiple configurations of CONFIG.SYS and AUTOEXEC.BAT files, a move clearly intended to provide greater flexibility. Unix has supported multiple configurations for years by allowing each user to specify a *.profile* file customized according to personal tastes. It became clear, though, that Microsoft was not interested in adopting the Unix approach, having chosen instead to tread down a path consisting primarily of GUIs based on Windows.

9.3   VMS: The antithesis of UNIX?

If MS-DOS was the king of the PC operating systems before Windows came along, Digital Equipment Corporation's VMS[3] was the king of minicomputer operating systems. Before Unix had caught the world's attention, no other single operating system in the minicomputer space had earned such a wide, loyal following.

---

3.   Digital later renamed VMS to "OpenVMS" in an attempt to fend off the aggressive marketing efforts of "open" (as in "Unix") systems vendors. Calling a closed system like VMS "open" was perhaps one of the ultimate ironies of its long and successful history.

VMS owed much of its success to Digital's VAX line of computers, where the same software could run unmodified on a range of systems from the desktop machine to the large, room-filling lab system. This compatibility at the binary level made it relatively easy to construct huge, fully integrated environments with a uniform style of interaction throughout.

Digital's approach to building systems was at one time the envy of the industry. What Digital had done with VMS and the VAX line had no equal in the minicomputer world. Other companies, such as IBM and Hewlett Packard, had tried to unify their entire product lines around a single architecture, but had failed. The success of Intel's x86 architecture running Windows is an affirmation of Digital's "one system one architecture" concept as well.

VMS was a closed-source, proprietary operating system, meaning a single company developed the source code, maintained a strong grip on it, and derived all profits from it. Although written by Digital's VMS Engineering Group in Nashua, New Hampshire, it really represented the aggregate thoughts on software that Digital's engineers had carried in their minds for years. The similarities to Digital's other operating systems were many. For instance, users of RSX-11, an earlier Digital operating system, felt very much at home with the VMS command interpreter. Like earlier Digital operating systems, VMS relied on compatibility across an entire hardware product line to strengthen and extend its user base.

The VMS developers had strong ideas about what constituted the VMS philosophy. Like the developers of the Atari Home Computer's operating system, they assumed not only that the user should be amply shielded from any vagaries lurking within the system, but that the user should be well informed of their existence. If the Atari approach was to build a tunnel through solid rock, then the VMS approach was to put lights in the tunnel.

Second, in the VMS environment, if big was good, then bigger was better. This led to the development of large, complex environments, such as Digital's All-In-1 office automation product, which integrated many closely related functions under a single user interface. VMS had been quite successful in this area and had one of the strongest office suites available before the PC-based ones came along.

A third element of the VMS philosophy was an artifact of the effect that the VMS mind set had on Digital's customers. Many people who purchased VMS did so because they had a defined task to accomplish and were unaware or unsure of the kind of information technology required to provide a solution. While the typical Linux user today says "I need this box" or "Give me that application," the typical VMS customer would ask, "How can I do this with your system?" The difference may appear subtle, but it profoundly affected how VMS engineers wrote software.

Applications developed by VMS engineers tended to be feature rich. But they were often rich under the covers, where the user couldn't see all of the wondrous complexity. The choice of features shown to the user at any one time was not very large, despite the fact that a large number of interesting options did exist. Unix and Linux applications designers usually make no such presumptions about what is interesting. The choices on a typical Unix system often include everything: the good, the bad, and that which may be safely ignored.

To a certain extent, an underlying belief of the VMS philosophy was that users are afraid of computers. Given the ubiquity of modern PC's, this might sound a little strange. The fact is, many people still feel threatened by computers. If they could, they would prefer to ignore the benefits of this exciting technology. Many wish that computers would simply go away.

Jon "maddog" Hall, a longtime proponent of Unix systems and more recently of Linux systems , has always asked a tough question: What about Mom and Pop? Mom and Pop, he would say, have a microwave oven, but use only 59 percent of its capabilities. They have a CD player, but don't know what quad oversampling is. They own a VCR and have yet to program it. They don't know what all the buttons on the remote do. In short, they refuse to learn about any technology that is not easy to use.

Mom and Pop—most Unix advocates hate to admit this and yet readily do so—would have a terrible time with the "have it your way" approach of Unix and Linux. Proponents of the VMS philosophy dealt with this notion a long time ago. The VMS developers were in the business of making the world's computers more accessible to those people who needed bounded solutions, not do-it-yourself toolkits.

Besides the obvious user interface differences, there were other ways in which VMS differed from Unix. Because they are at opposite ends of the spectrum in so many respects, one could claim that VMS was really the antithesis of Unix. For example, VMS usually provided a single path to a solution; Unix often provides a dozen ways or more. VMS tended toward large, monolithic programs with lots of options to accommodate the vast general user population; Unix leans toward small programs, each of which performs a single function with a limited set of options. VMS was originally written in assembly language and BLISS-32, languages highly tuned for the underlying hardware

Through the Glass Darkly: Linux vs. Windows

Just because you have an army of people saying that you're right doesn't mean that you're right. I can go out and get an army of people to say I'm right, too.
From a conversation with Don "Smokey" Wallace

In the previous chapter, we compared Linux and the Unix philosophy with the philosophies of other operating systems. While those systems were significant in their own right, they have not have the kind of impact on the world that Microsoft Windows has had. We explored those systems for good reason, however. Not only did they exhibit characteristics common to proprietary systems, but they embodied design philosophies that run counter to the Unix philosophy in various ways. And, not surprisingly, adherents of those design philosophies have found a new system that continues their approaches in Microsoft Windows.

If you'll carefully examine the design philosophy behind Microsoft Windows, you'll find that it bears strong resemblance to Digital's VMS operating system. This is not an accident. Their roots are similar because of the design approach taken by David Cutler, the lead engineer from Digital who was responsible for making VMS (and Digital's VAX hardware) successful. Cutler was the driving force behind most of Digital's operating systems down through the years, and VMS was his magnum opus. Or so it would seem. Soon after VMS reached its zenith in the early 1990s, however, Cutler sought kindred spirits elsewhere. He found them in the offices of Microsoft, where he led the design of what eventually became Windows NT, a system that ultimately garnered much greater market share than VMS.

At the time, there was a lot of speculation about whether Windows NT was really the next version of VMS. In fact, when someone pointed out that the letters "W-N-T" are the next letters in the alphabet after "V-M-S," Cutler was rumored to have replied, "What took you so long?"[1]

This is not to say that Cutler heavily influenced the graphical style of interaction of Microsoft Windows. Microsoft had embarked upon the GUI path long before Cutler's arrival. The Windows GUI aside, however, Windows resembles VMS in many ways. Windows is a closed-source, proprietary operating system. Despite numerous calls from its business partners and competitors alike, Microsoft has never released the innermost workings of the Windows operating system. Even if it does yield to market or legal pressure someday, it's doubtful that it will ever release all of the Windows source code. The company acts as though it believes that the Windows source code is the technological equivalent of the family jewels and should be carefully guarded. Whether right or wrong, it appears to hold the belief that by making the

---

1.   *The Computists' Communique*, Vol. 2, No. 26, June 24, 1992.

Windows source code publicly available, it will give away its competitive advantage.[2]

The makers of the Windows OS also hold to the "bigger is better" approach to software design. Rather than build software as a collection of smaller programs integrated in interesting new ways, they prefer to release increasingly larger, monolithic programs that often suffer from bloat and consume enormous amounts of system resources.

The Microsoft Office suite is one example of such a product. Rather than containing a series of plug-in modules that could be inserted as needed, it tries to load "everything but the kitchen sink" when it starts up. This has led to the need for systems requiring progressively larger amounts of memory. While this hungry consumption of system resources delights memory chip foundries, it forces users to spend money on memory and CPU upgrades that would generally be unnecessary with more efficient applications. Linux, by comparison, has already proven far more frugal in its consumption of resources, largely because of its modular architecture. While any operating system can obviously benefit from huge amounts of memory, Linux can still operate effectively in systems having a fraction of the resources that Windows requires.

Windows most resembles VMS, however, in its design philosophy with respect to the user's fear of computers. Recall that the VMS developers assumed that users consider the computer something to be feared. In designing software for Windows, software developers must go out of their way to make the operating system easier to use *for the novice user*.

This is a fundamental difference between the Windows and Unix philosophies. Remember that Unix makes no attempt to satisfy the ease-of-use concerns of novice users. Its textual user interface, with its many ways of accomplishing tasks, remains stubbornly resistant to quick absorption by novices. Users must embark upon a comparatively steep learning curve in order to take advantage of its inherent power. They must spend days, weeks, or even months becoming proficient enough with Unix to perform some tasks that can be learned and executed within minutes on a Windows-based system.

---

2.   Microsoft has made the Windows source code available in read-only form to its partners from time to time. But Microsoft rarely allows any other company to make changes. Microsoft normally makes all the modifications.

Linux attempts to bridge this gap between the novice and the expert user by providing a choice of GUIs such as the KDE and Gnome desktop environments. KDE and Gnome provide Windows-like user interfaces that offer the usual "point-and-click" features and add a few new wrinkles of their own. They form a shield protecting the user from many underlying commands, usually limiting the available options to those best utilized by novice to intermediate users. Experienced users can access the really complex stuff only via text-based, command-line interfaces.

Because of its tremendous flexibility, Linux allows you to operate in a dual world where text-based and graphical user interfaces coexist. It begs an important question, however. Although Linux may provide a Windows-like environment, why not run Windows and get the real thing? If you already have Windows, why would you need something that is almost Windows? As the song says, "Ain't nothing like the real thing, baby!"

One answer is that while the Linux and Windows desktops may look similar, there exists a significant architectural difference between the two —namely, that the Windows GUI is tightly integrated with the underlying operating system. Unlike the X Window System found on Linux—which is just another application program running under the operating system— the Windows GUI and the operating system are effectively a single entity. They are so tightly coupled that any error occuring in the GUI can have disastrous consequences for the operating system. If the GUI should hang for some reason, there is no other way for the user to take control of the system. Virtually all interactions between the user and the operating system are expected to occur via the GUI. There is no other way for the user to operate a Windows system except through the GUI. Contrast this with Linux, where the X Window System could easily be replaced with an entirely different user interface. In fact, the Linux Gnome and KDE environments are exactly that—different desktop interfaces layered on top of the same operating system.

The division between the GUI and the operating system is really the age-old split between form and function. The *function* is the content of the matter (i.e., what you're trying to say). It is the reason that the application exists. The *form* represents how it is presented to the viewer. The form is important as it helps deliver the message in a manner palatable to the viewer. But without the function, or content, of the message, the form is an empty blast of hot air. With respect to operating systems, a flashy GUI is meaningless unless you're delivering the functional capabilities that the user desires. In other words, content rules.

10.1   It's the content, stupid!

If you were born after the late 1970s, your first meaningful encounter with a computer was probably with a WIMPy (*W*indows, *I*cons, *M*enus, *P*ointers) personal computer. Your computer has always had a GUI where you would point at and click on small graphical images called icons. As far as you're concerned, Microsoft invented windows and menus and all the visual delights that make PCs so much fun.

The truth is that Microsoft didn't invent the WIMP user interface after all. Xerox—yes, the copier people—did. The Xerox Star, introduced in 1981 by Xerox's Palo Alto Research Center (a.k.a. "Xerox PARC") was the first significant release of a product with a WIMP user interface. Other early systems, such as Smalltalk and the Alto, embodied some of the ideas found in the Star, but in the Star, the developers brought all of the elements together for the first time.

Many aspects of the Star system can still be seen in Microsoft Windows, the Apple Macintosh, and the various Linux GUI environments available today. The desktop metaphor, where the user is invited to view the screen objects as objects found on top of one's office desk, came from the Star. The use of bit-mapped displays, icons, and the mouse all originated in the Star's user interface.

Microsoft did not invent the World Wide Web, either. Tim Berners-Lee holds that distinction. His vision for the Web was based not on dreams of becoming a wealthy information czar, but on a sincere desire to see people communicate better. He and Robert Cailliau began implementing his vision by writing a simple, no-frills Web browser in 1990 at CERN, the European physics laboratory straddling the French-Swiss border.[3]

The WIMP user interface and the World Wide Web exist primarily for one reason: content. The Star's bit-mapped display brought us the ability to display photographs, animations, video, and more readable text. The Web gave us the means to move the data from powerful servers to the user's machine for display. The combination of these two technologies facilitated the delivery of rich content to the desktop.

---

3.   "The Man Who Invented the Web," *Time*, Vol. 149, No. 20, May 19, 1997. For more on the history of the Web, go to http://www.cern.ch.

In the early days of AltaVista, the first "super search engine" of the Web, the developers were fond of saying, "It's the content, stupid!" What they meant by this was that it doesn't matter whether you have the fastest search engine, the brightest graphics, or the flashiest desktop. Users will be impressed with flash and glitter for only so long. Eventually, you must provide information that meets the needs of the individual. Otherwise, the user will look elsewhere. If you don't have content of real value, you have nothing.

While Microsoft Windows helps deliver content to the desktop, Microsoft doesn't create the content. Others generate the content: the syndicated news services, the film studios, the independent producers, and the millions of users of word processors, spreadsheets, and graphical editors. Windows only provides the vehicle to deliver that content. For all its flashy GUI and slick desktop, Windows provides the sizzle, but it doesn't provide the steak. The steak, in this case, is the application's content. How you deliver the content *is* important, of course. But the GUI's importance is dwarfed by the content that you're trying to deliver.

Indeed, content rules. In fact, content is so important that even if computers didn't exist, the producers would still find a way to get it to you. In the beginning, content passed from village to village by word of mouth. With the invention of the printing press, content passed from city to city by the written word in the form of books and newspapers. Later on, radio and television became the media for delivering content to huge masses of people. The World Wide Web and the Internet are merely the next means of delivering the all-important content.

If Microsoft, Linux, and the Web didn't exist, the content would still find its way to you. It's that important. One way or another, if the information matters, you will get it. There are people who have commercial or ideological reasons for seeing to it that it does. And they will use whatever means is available to get it to you.

So whether or not a GUI is available is of secondary importance. What counts is the information being conveyed. If you are not seeing the content that matters to you, you will send the messenger on his way and look for the next messenger.

But aren't some kinds of delivery mechanisms better at delivering content than others? In a word, yes. While you may be tempted to think that video has no equal, however, you may be surprised to learn that it pales in comparison to the power of the written word, even in this day and age.

Let's take a look at the three main delivery mechanisms: visual, audible, and textual. By examining these, it is hoped that you will begin to understand why Unix, which is primarily a text-oriented system, is still incredibly powerful, even in the age of CNN and MTV.

Let's start by looking at the visual media first, the least powerful of the three. *Huh? What do you mean, "the least powerful of the three"? Everyone knows the power of video.* Stick with me for a minute. You may think differently in a page or so. Keep in mind that we're driving to a conclusion about Windows—a visual type of operating system—versus Unix, a text-oriented operating system.

10.1.1 Visual content: "I seen it with my own eyes."

No doubt about it; the visual media are powerful indeed. They are particularly adept at evoking emotion in the viewer. When you see something, it's as if a bond takes place between you and the scene on the screen or page. Whether in a positive or negative way, most visuals will cause you to respond in an emotional fashion.

There are two kinds of visual media, *static* and *dynamic*. *Static* visual media are drawings and photographs. In the age of the World Wide Web and the Internet, static images abound. Nearly every Web site that one visits contains static images. Many of the large commercial sites display so-called "banner ads," commercial graphics designed to lure you into clicking on them to whisk you away to another Web site where you're likely to spend money on a product or service that you have been selected to receive information about by virtue of your demographic makeup.

Static images are normally easy to produce, making them a relatively inexpensive medium. Photos can be quickly captured these days with digital cameras or as static frames obtained from video sources. Other graphics can be produced using common graphics applications such as Adobe's Photoshop® or the popular open-source application known as "The Gimp."

One drawback to static images is that they can be difficult to catalog and retrieve without some sort of textual explanation of their content. For example, if you were told to locate a photograph of a lumberjack chopping down a tree, you could spend a long time poring over thousands of photos to find one. Large stock photo services make this task much easier by providing text descriptions of photo contents. Consumers of these services then search through the text descriptions—usually with the aid of a sophisticated search engine—to locate the photos they are interested in.

On the typical computer desktop screen, static images are often used as icons to represent a function to perform or an object to be manipulated. Because people can normally recognize images faster than they can recognize text, users often find that the icons accelerate their performance when using GUIs. The problem is, until you have some idea as to what the icons represent, the icons can actually slow you down. You may even find yourself referring to the text accompanying the icon to describe its purpose.

Dynamic visual media today largely consist of video and, to a lesser extent, film. While film and video have obviously been hugely successful with the introduction of the motion picture and television, they haven't had quite the impact on the written word that some predicted they would. While many people prefer to watch the evening news on television, for example, surprising numbers of people still prefer to read a newspaper or magazine article. And although television has long held the top role as entertainer in many households, it is beginning to lose ground to more interactive pursuits, as new forms of Internet-based entertainment become available. Video may have killed the radio star, but on-demand forms of interaction are now killing the television star.

Although static images are relatively cheap to produce, video has proven to be prohibitively expensive to produce at more than rudimentary levels of quality. It often takes large amounts of computing power and storage to produce even short video segments. Putting together reasonable video presentations takes a level of skill that goes beyond that required to operate a still camera. Also, with today's video formats, a two-hour film requires more than 500 MB of storage. Contrast this with static images; hundreds or even thousands of images can be stored in less than a gigabyte of space.

Video still has the same drawbacks as static images when it comes to cataloging and retrieving video clips. Some sort of textual representation is still required to make it easier to retrieve video clips on particular topics. The problem is compounded further by the large amounts of storage required for the actual video clips. Imagine if one had a library of 100,000 video clips without labels. Locating one that shows clever animals outsmarting stupid people would be an arduous task.

It should be evident thus far that while visual media can be powerful and dynamic, they still require "backup" assistance from textual representations.

160

Without the text used for purposes of search and retrieval, producing images and videos would be a labor-intensive process and the costs would soar. Hence, the amount of video available would be reduced to a small trickle without textual representation. While the text used to label the visual media isn't quite as "good" as the visuals, it is cheap and effective. It's the "worse is better" idea again that we spoke of in an earlier chapter. Hmmmm. Maybe there's a pattern here? Picture that in your mind while we move on to audible content.

10.1.2 Audible content: "Can you hear me now?"

Audible content, another component of multimedia, has been around longer than video but not quite as long as static visual media. It consists of *raw audio, music,* and *the spoken word.* Let's take a (brief) look at each of these.

Raw audio represents any of the innumerable sounds that the human ear can perceive. Many of these have been captured on magnetic tape or digitized and stored as audio files on computers. Often referred to as "sound bites," they can be anything from the frantic blasts of a gunfight in East L.A. to the almost imperceptible sounds of stillness on a mountain lake at sunrise.

To add more words to the audible content known as *music* would only be redundant. Music is a communications medium that traverses international boundaries and generation gaps as easily as one steps over cracks in a sidewalk. Many volumes have been written about music, as something both to create and to enjoy.

Music shares many of the same characteristics as visual content. It can be relatively inexpensive to produce—especially in the case of live performances—or it can be painstakingly recorded and engineered in a studio using equipment costing huge sums of money. With both visual and audible content, the quality often depends on the amount of money one is willing to spend.

Music also shares the ability of visual content to communicate emotion to the individual. Just as people often associate feelings of joy, fear, or sadness with particular motion pictures, so do people associate similar feelings with favorite songs heard down through the years. And with so many motion pictures these days containing songs by popular artists on their soundtracks, the line between the two continues to blur with each passing year.

Finally, the *spoken word* consists of audible content that could be represented in textual form. The spoken word can be anything from news broadcasts and radio talk shows to historic speeches. It frequently appears in situations where listeners find their time divided between absorbing the spoken word and completing some other task, such as commuting or doing household chores. Information that is carried in print media frequently crosses over to the spoken word, so that the same information found in, say, a newspaper such as *USA Today* will also be detailed in local and national news broadcasts.

One disadvantage of the spoken word is that it is language-sensitive. The speaker must speak the same language—in some cases the same dialect of the language—as the listener. Otherwise, little communication occurs, and the value of the spoken word is greatly diminished. Even worse, in some instances, the spoken word can be culturally biased, as words can have different meanings depending on the context and the background of both the listener and the speaker. Human-based translation services do exist, but the cost of good interpreters and the immediacy of the spoken word often preclude the translation of most spoken content into one's native tongue.

All three types of audible content share a common need for cataloging and categorization in order to be useful. All musical productions, sound sites, and recorded speeches must be documented in some sort of textual medium that allows for reasonably rapid retrieval. For example, suppose one had a collection of a thousand musical compositions on compact discs without labels. One can only imagine the amount of frustration one would have in seeking out the particular piece one was interested in listening to at any given time. The text labels, even if they are worn or barely legible, help classify the contents of each compact disc.

Should the music be stored on another medium, such as on a personal computer, the same text-cataloging requirement still exists. Suppose that instead of a collection of compact discs, one had stored the 10,000 songs on a computer as a set of files with similar names. This obviously would not be very useful. By comparison, if the names of all the songs were stored as a list in a flat ASCII file or a simple database, locating your favorite song would be a simple task. Whether the catalog text data is printed on labels or stored in a database, the value of such data cannot be overstated.

It should be evident by this point that while the visual and audible media are powerful conveyors of imagery and emotions, they cannot stand alone.

They need assistance from textual data catalogs once the amount of content exceeds, say, several dozen pieces. Indeed, without textual representations used to identify those media, the number of films, speeches, and musical compositions within your grasp would be limited to a minuscule fraction of what is available today. Text is a fundamental enabler for audio and video media. That's why text is the most powerful form of content of all.

10.1.3 Textual content: "Video killed the radio star, but it couldn't kill the tabloids."

While visual and audible content have emotional impact, it is the written word that keeps us coming back for more. A Web site may have glitzy graphics and the coolest sounds, but these will not hold your interest forever. Unless a site has good written content of interest to you, you will not stay for long, and you won't be back again.

Many people believed that once the television came along, it would be the end of radio. For the most part, radio has succumbed to the onslaught of television. No longer do people rush home to listen to the latest radio broadcast. They might listen to news on their car radio, but only until they can get home and turn on CNN or watch their favorite television show. Radio simply doesn't hold the appeal that it once did. Why get half the picture on the radio when you can get all of it on video?

While video has all but killed the radio star, video is finding its dominance usurped by a still more powerful medium—the Internet. The same people who used to watch television for hours at a time are finding that they are equally addicted to the interactive aspect of the World Wide Web, perhaps even more so. And what is the most popular form of content on the Web? Here's a clue. It's not music files (although these are indeed popular), and it's not video clips. It's text, pure and simple.

The reason people flock to the Internet and the World Wide Web is to absorb textual content. The Web is the largest library in the history of mankind, and it's ever-changing. Whatever your interests, no matter how obscure, you're liable to find something about it somewhere on the Web. And nearly all of the content is text. For every video clip or music file, there are thousands of Web pages containing minimal graphics and lots of text.

Text rules. Why? Despite the onslaught of radio, films and television, newspapers exist and are still flourishing. While everyone first thought that the computer would turn our world into a paperless society, people today find that the amount of junk mail arriving daily is a testament to the fact that textual matter—both printed and online—is alive and well and growing in your mail box faster than Caltiki, the Immortal Monster.[4] Let's take a look at some of the reasons why text content is so powerful and why it has continued to flourish over the years.

Text is an inexpensive way to store and transmit ideas. In terms of storage space required, text is considerably more compact than audio or video. For example, this entire book fits in less than 1 MB of space. It costs a fraction of a cent to store it on a CD or DVD. If I were to record the book as an audio book, the amount of storage required would be hundreds of times more than that required by the text files. As a video presentation, it would be even more costly.

Transmittal of textual content across networks is also inexpensive. Even as network bandwidth improves, textual material will always be less expensive to transmit because of the vast difference in size between text files and audio or video files. On a fast network, this entire book can be transmitted in a fraction of a second. Other forms of content take longer, possibly substantially longer, depending on the sizes of the files and the network throughput rate.

For the 2002 Winter Olympics in Salt Lake City, Qwest Communications built a network with a capacity of more than 388 trillion bits per second.[5] To put it into perspective, that's the equivalent of transmitting the entire U.S. Library of Congress—currently more than 17 million volumes —*twice* per second. With network capacity like that, it is theoretically possible to transmit all of the world's books in a few minutes (or less!). Audio and video aren't nearly as efficient. With textual content, you never have to worry about having enough bandwidth.

Text can be indexed and searched highly efficiently. What good is the ability to transmit at 2 LOCS (*L*ibraries *O*f *C*ongress per *S*econd) unless you know what book to look in? Here is where today's ultrafast, gargantuan text search engines come in. As of this writing, Google, the popular Internet search engine, indexes more than 2 billion Web pages, over 700 million Usenet forum messages, and over 35 million non-HTML (i.e., non–Web page) documents. Despite quantities like these, with a little forethought one can locate most needles in this megahaystack in a few seconds or so. Try doing *that* with

---

4.   Check out *Caltiki, the Immortal Monster* on the Internet Movie Database at, http://www.imdb.com!

5.   *Telephony*, January 14, 2002.

your family's 2-billion-page photo album. Images may be interesting to look at, but you'll never find them very fast without text.

Google also bears a closer look for its technical architecture. Interestingly, Google doesn't employ huge RISC servers from the major Unix system vendors. It uses more than 10,000 off-brand Intel-based PCs running Linux in a cluster arrangement. The PCs are rack-mounted and connected by 100-Mbps network links. So the world's fastest text search engine runs on a large array of cheap, small PCs using a free, open-source operating system.

Not only is smaller better, it's cheaper, too. The calculation of Microsoft Windows license fees for 10,000 PCs is left as an exercise for the reader.

An interesting feature of Google and other major text search engines is that they offer instant machine translations of foreign-language pages into many other languages. The KDE Konqueror Web browser found on Linux even has a "translate this page" menu option that goes to the AltaVista Web site and translates your current page from and to all of the popular languages. But wait; we're getting ahead of ourselves here.

Text can be inexpensively machine-translated into other languages. Machine translation of text has been the Holy Grail of linguists since as far back as the seventeenth century. The idea of automatically translating text from a foreign language to your own has been the subject of countless science-fiction stories down through the years. It wasn't until the latter part of the twentieth century, however, that it became not only possible, but practical. Powerful servers on the Internet have made machine-translated text a commodity today. Virtually all of the major search engines provide a means of translating the contents of Web pages between the most popular Western languages and even a few Asian ones. Science fiction, as in many other cases, has become science fact.

Machine translation (MT in linguistic lingo) is far from perfect. But relative to the cost of having a human translator at your beck and call during all hours of the day, MT is cheap and effective. It doesn't offer the same level of accuracy as a human translator. It's particularly ineffective in dealing with idiomatic expressions in most languages unless the expressions are handled explicitly. So in a sense, MT is worse than human translation. But what have we said before about cheap and effective things? That's right. Worse is better.

What about motion pictures? Does text have an advantage over audible and visual content in this case? Doesn't one get some idea of what a foreign film is about by watching the moves and expressions of the characters? That's partly true. Once again, video and audio tend to be fairly good at transmitting emotion. But to really understand the subtleties of what is happening in, say, *Wo hu cang long* (*Crouching Tiger, Hidden Dragon*), one has to read the subtitles. Again, text rules. It holds the key to understanding.

Text can be very precise in its meanings. The first time one sets one's eyes on a new GUI, one becomes acutely aware of the fact that icons and images are very imprecise means of identifying objects. If you've seen similar GUIs in the past, the knowledge of what the icons and images on the screen represent is transferable. You won't have much difficulty identifying word processor documents, programs, and so on. Icons and images are optimally useful in helping you quickly identify *what* you have.

Unfortunately, icons by themselves provide only a symbolic representation of something. Problems occur when you have more than one of those somethings and you need to locate a specific instance. At that point, you need an identifier more concrete than a set of pictures that all look the same. You may be able to remember that clicking on the document icon on the left brings up your doctoral thesis and clicking on the document icon on the right brings up a collection of jokes from your buddies. But can you remember when you have a folder containing, say, a dozen similar icons? How useful would it be if your favorite Internet search engine returned two hundred document icons per page as a result of searching for "Linux kernel"? You would gladly pay $50 for a "Get Out of (Icon) Hell Free" card long before you finished viewing the other two million items returned.

Icons and images can be useful with direct manipulation user interfaces (e.g., Microsoft Windows), as long you're working with a very small data set. When you have more than a dozen files or so, you need text captions on the icons to help you identify the contents of the files. The captions eventually become more important than the icons themselves. Experienced Windows users usually set their "Explorer" or file manager–type application to display lists of file names instead of large icons.

The Windows folder-type views of file trees are especially cumbersome. This is an unfortunate irony, as the file-tree abstraction works quite well in both the Unix and Windows worlds. In the Windows case, navigating a file tree by clicking on icons can be very time-consuming as one drills progressively deeper. Linux and Unix power users find that the preciseness of text is a bonus here, as a textual representation of the file tree can easily be fed into a simple search command such as *grep*:

```
find . | grep myfile
```

In this case, the *find* command returns a list of all files and folders contained in the current folder. The *find* command operates recursively, so it will open all folders in the directory and all folders found within those, ad infinitum. The *grep* command selects the file name or names in the list containing the string "myfile."

The foregoing command has a distinct advantage with file paths that are broad and deep, such as */home/mike/eventcalendar/2004/May/19/Bahamas/Freeport/Princess/Towers.txt*. By specifying "Towers.txt" instead of "myfile" you would locate the file very quickly. Of course, Unix allows you to use the results of a command or set of commands as the input to another command. Here is a quick way to locate and edit the "Towers.txt" file under Unix:

```
vi `find . | grep Towers.txt`
```

To perform the equivalent action under Windows, you would have to start at the "/home" folder and drill down through each successive folder until you found the "Towers.txt" file. Then you would have to invoke a word processor on the file. Now imagine if each folder contained not a dozen but hundreds of files. It would be a tedious task indeed to navigate through each one until you found the right folder path leading to the desired file.[6]

And if this technique weren't fast enough, consider the Linux *locate* command. It works almost identically to the *find* command, except that it uses a database containing an index of reference pointers to locate files and folders virtually instantaneously. One can locate files hiding in stacks of thousands of files in a fraction of a second.

By using text instead of icons and a GUI, you can deal easily with trees of arbitrary width and depth. This is not to say that you cannot operate on large trees under Windows. They're simply more cumbersome under Windows. As the size of the data set increases, clicking through more and more objects becomes an arduous task. The use of text, on the other hand, allows you to be very precise in specifying what to access, even if it is nested many levels deep.

People who are not familiar with this concept often shake their heads in disbelief when they see experienced Linux users typing away at their keyboards with only terminal windows visible on their screens. They regard them as rel-

---

6.   Yes, you *could* use the "Find Files or Folders" option under Windows Explorer to find "Towers.txt." In the time it would take you to fill in the blank in the dialog box, the Linux user could have invoked the *vi* text editor on the file. The extra steps of moving back and forth between the keyboard and the mouse slow you down.

ics from the dinosaur days of terminals and teletypes. They wonder why in this day and age that these Neanderthals aren't using a mouse and clicking on icons like their Windows counterparts.

The answer is quite simple. Text gets you there faster. Sooner or later, Linux users eventually resort to using text in terminal windows because that's where the power is. One can only click on icons and images so fast. Beyond that, the preciseness afforded by text is too much of an advantage to overlook. This is not to say that Linux users never click on icons in the KDE or Gnome graphical user environments. It's just that when one needs to operate quickly and efficiently, GUIs are simply not fast enough.

As Windows users become "power users," they must click faster. Linux "power users," on the other hand, simply type less to do more. Hmmm. Click faster? Or type less? You decide.

Text is more efficient at dealing with large amounts of content because of data abstraction. A common technique with icons is to present a miniature representation of a larger image. By glancing at the iconic version of the image, you have some idea of what the full-size image will look like. Text has no direct equivalent of this kind of representation. However, it has something much better.

For example, suppose you use a textual description of a file path that looks something like this:

```
/home/mike/files/documents/financial/tax_returns/2002/
   return.tax
```

It takes an instant for you to determine that the file path represents my 2002 income tax return. Furthermore, the path suggests that (1) this is likely to be one of many tax returns stored on the system, (2) I probably have stored more than one kind of financial document, (3) I may be keeping more than one kind of document in general, (4) I may be keeping other kinds of files besides documents, (5) there may be other users on the system whose files are stored there, and (6) the */home* area on the system is where most of the users' files are kept.

That's a fair amount of information that you can glean from the file path. If you tried to represent the equivalent graphically (and without text altogether), you would have a very difficult time as you tried to show different icons for each component in the file path. The user would have a difficult time remembering what each icon represented. One would ultimately resort to attaching a textual description of each icon as an aid to help the user identify the specifics of what the icon represents. Of course, at that point, the user is back to using textual content again.

We could go on forever here with examples of data abstraction using textual representation, but I think you already get the picture. (No pun intended.) Graphical representations using icons or images are woefully inadequate for the purposes of categorizing and abstracting data.

As we've seen in the last few pages, audio and visual content, while emotionally engaging, play secondary roles in our use of computing systems. For virtually all primary tasks, text is second to none. The greatest amount of computer systems usage centers on textual content. Without textual content, most computers would be pretty playthings of little use in our lives.

But why is this so important in comparing Unix and its variants with Microsoft Windows? It is because Windows is primarily a visual system, with all that that entails. Microsoft has, in so many words (again, no pun intended), said so. Graphical user-computer interaction represents one of the core elements of the Windows philosophy.

Unix and its variants derive their power from their ability as text-processing systems. Text is the most powerful kind of content, and the typical Unix or Linux distribution has hundreds of programs designed to access, create, and manipulate it. There is no other system in the world as capable of dealing with text as Unix.

Thus far in this chapter, we have learned about the philosophy of Microsoft Windows as a graphically oriented operating system. We have seen that GUIs, while initially useful for helping people overcome their fear of computers, pose real problems as the size of the data set increases and novice users become power users. Visual operating systems can actually hamper the user in his or her never-ending quest for content as text becomes one's medium of choice.

This is not to say that GUIs are inherently evil. They serve their purpose and can be quite handy at times. The key difference between Unix and Linux versus Windows is in how they are implemented. With Windows, the GUI is *the* way to interact with the system. With Unix and Linux, the GUI is *one* way to interact with the system. Therein lies the difference.

Having built a foundation of general understanding, it's time to reexamine the specific tenets of the Unix philosophy and see how Windows relates —or doesn't relate—to them, as the case may be. This part is going to be a bit of a whirlwind tour. By now, you probably realize how Windows stacks up, and we'll just go over some of the finer points.

Tenet 1: Small is beautiful

Back in the early days of Windows 3.1, Microsoft Windows was a small GUI layered over an even smaller MS-DOS. Over time, however, it grew into a behemoth of massive proportions. Even with shared libraries, which are supposed to help reduce the amount of space consumed, applications such as Microsoft Office and Internet Explorer have now earned the popular nickname "bloatware" because of their overwhelming size. If you think they must be so large because they offer so many features, I would invite you to refer back to the discussion about the Three Systems of Man. These are excellent examples of applications suffering from "Second System Syndrome." When Microsoft finally realizes that these applications need to grow smaller instead of larger, it will have embarked upon the path to the Third System, which we've determined to be best of the three. In the meantime, we need to plow through hundreds of features that do little to enhance our ability to perform the core tasks for which these applications were intended.

Tenet 2: Make each program do one thing well

This tenet speaks of the small-tools or component approach to computing. While Microsoft's technologies such as OLE and ActiveX are component approaches as well, they differ in one significant aspect. Unix components are designed to be manipulated and integrated *by the user*. While Microsoft goes out of its way to hide the fact that the components exist, the Unix approach is to inform the user of the components and encourage him or her to exploit them to their fullest. The Windows approach to components is a reflection of the mistaken idea that users fear computers and that they should not be exposed to their inner workings.

Tenet 3: Build a prototype as soon as possible

Microsoft earns high marks in this regard, as its tools (e.g., Visual Studio and other IDEs) facilitate rapid prototyping. I once attended a presentation by a Microsoft sales engineer who demonstrated that it is easy to create a simple, Web-based database application in as little as five minutes using Microsoft tools. Building a prototype in five minutes leaves plenty of time for user discussions on how best to refine the application. Note that in this regard,

Microsoft has parted ways with the VMS approach in which designs must be thoroughly reviewed before a stitch of code is written. I'm not afraid to give credit where credit is due.

Tenet 4: Choose portability over efficiency

There's a reason why it's called the "Wintel" monopoly. For years, the various Microsoft Windows operating systems were strongly wedded to the Intel x86 CPU line. In the interest of making its ever-burgeoning GUI run at peak efficiency, Microsoft needed to stay closely coupled to Intel hardware. With the introduction of Windows NT, Microsoft finally saw the value of portability. NT ran on four architectures: Intel x86, DEC Alpha, MIPS R4400, and the Motorola PowerPC. Windows XP, however, in a big step backwards, runs on only the Intel x86 architecture, while Linux runs on all architectures available today. Has Microsoft truly learned the value of portability over efficiency? If Windows XP is any indication, it's doubtful.

Tenet 5: Store data in flat text files

Microsoft gets failing marks in this area. While some Windows system configuration files are stored as ASCII text, by and large the Microsoft world is still one where the hidden nature of binary files is cherished and adored. For example, Windows stores critical configuration information in the registry, a binary formatted file vulnerable to corruption. Proponents of various open-source initiatives, such as Richard Stallman of the Free Software Foundation, have rightfully criticized Microsoft for persisting in the use of binary file formats for Microsoft Word, Excel, and other key applications. The trend in file formats is clearly toward some form of (Extensible Markup Language) XML in all areas, which is a text-based format. As of this writing, Microsoft has plans to change the Office binary file formats to XML. Linux-based office tools, on the other hand, have been XML-based for several years already.

Tenet 6: Use software leverage to your advantage

How can a corporation that adheres to a closed-source, proprietary philosophy ever take advantage of software leverage? Well, one way would be for Microsoft to absorb the software ideas produced by various open-source development efforts and incorporate them into its products. It has done this, oftentimes to its benefit. But software leverage, to be used most advantageously, is a two-way street. Microsoft needs to allow others to leverage its source code easily. And this means opening up the Windows source code for others to use and improve. The result would be a plethora of new Windows applications, most of which would probably be available on both Windows and Linux. We've already discussed the likelihood of this happening.

Tenet 7: Use shell scripts to increase leverage and portability

In order to use shell scripts, you must have a shell command interpreter. Microsoft has a few, such as the Windows Scripting Host and its MS-DOS batch mechanism. And due to the resourcefulness of the Perl fans (or is it fanatics?) of this world, Perl is available on Microsoft platforms as well. The problem is that Windows Scripting Host and MS-DOS batch files have a very limited command set to draw from, while Perl has an extensive set of modules to incorporate if you want to take the time to track them down and install them. But plain vanilla Windows has little to offer in terms of a good scripting environment. So users typically default to using the GUI to interact with the system. This means Windows will be able to perform only those tasks that someone has had the forethought to write a GUI application for. Scriptable operations—especially those typically thought of on the spur of the moment —simply won't exist.

This has an impact on the ability of Windows programs to run at optimum speed. GUI applications require you to click on buttons and make selections from list boxes from time to time, forcing programs to interact with a human being instead of another program. As we've discussed earlier, this interaction becomes a blocking factor for optimum performance. Unless a program is designed to operate without human intervention, it can run only as fast as a person can press a mouse button. Most Unix programs, on the other hand, can be driven by scripts that are limited only by the speed of the machine.

One might argue that an operating system that runs without human intervention is just a server. For that reason, some pundits have tried to downplay Linux's potential as a mainstream operating system and instead relegate it to the supposedly less interesting server role. They say that Windows' "superior" GUI will continue to rule the desktop. These critics are missing the point. Because Linux is an outstanding server, it is more capable at *all* aspects of computing, including the desktop. A properly constructed desktop environment is simply another task for a server. One need only look at the number of desktop environments available under Linux to realize that Linux has already become a first-rate desktop server.

Tenet 8: Avoid captive user interfaces

By their very nature, GUIs are CUIs. They tend to transfix the user's attention and not release the person to do other things until he has satisfied the input requirements of the application, whether it be choosing from a list of options or clicking on an "OK" button. Windows systems get around this problem by allowing the user to open multiple windows concurrently, thereby providing the ability to interact with more than one application simultaneously. So, at least in this regard, a window system—any window system—pays lip service to the tenet of avoiding CUIs.

Many Windows applications (but not all, thankfully) have been written with the assumption that the user wants to interact with only one application. They overlook the fact that, while Windows is a graphical user environment, it is also a *windowing* environment, where multiple applications may be contending for the user's attention at any given time. A most blatant example of this is a pop-up dialog box that commands the user to interact with it alone until one has clicked on something in the box. This type of dialog box is called a "modal" dialog. Many modern Windows applications, especially those written since the start of the new millennium, have become more sensitive to the plight of the user who needs to interact with multiple applications to accomplish a given task and have avoided using modal dialogs. However, remnants of this older style of interaction still exist.

One way to avoid the kind of thinking that leads to CUIs is to think in terms of clients communicating with servers. The KDE Desktop Communications Protocol (DCOP) demonstrates just that kind of thinking. Developed by KDE developers Matthias Ettrich and Preston Brown, DCOP forms the basis for a generic interprocess communication facility.[7] What makes DCOP different is that while other interprocess communications protocols (e.g., RMI) deal with nonhuman communication, DCOP is a foundation of the KDE desktop environment, the chief purpose of which is human-computer interaction. With DCOP, programs can easily communicate with other programs via standard APIs, many of which offer GUIs. However, because any program that understands the DCOP protocol can be used in the

---

7.   See http://developer.kde.org, *KDE 3.0 Architecture*

KDE user environment, it opens up the possibility of scripting tools that can drive desktop objects and applications. In the case of DCOP, a KDE client doesn't really need to know what is communicating with it as long it speaks DCOP.

If you're thinking that this sounds remarkably close to the notion that "all programs are filters." you're getting the idea. Whether the communication method is a Unix pipe or a DCOP connection, it's still the same approach. Small programs are once again talking to other small programs.

I could go on a rant here about how Windows doesn't accommodate this kind of scripting easily, but I have a sense that I would only be preaching to the growing chorus of KDE developers who have found a better way to build a desktop environment. It is, however, a great lead-in to the next tenet.

Tenet 9: Make every program a filter

This tenet is a foreign notion to the Windows world in general. The Windows approach tends to be "let's build a really big program with a gazillion features and it will sell really well if we market it cleverly enough." One can build a huge software conglomerate by selling products like these and still not get it right. Applications like Microsoft Outlook don't interface very well with other programs because the developers were not thinking in terms of programs as filters. Contrast this with the MH mail handler we discussed earlier. MH, too, has a comprehensive set of features. But users and developers can easily add new components to the MH suite, while Outlook is a large but limited environment. It doesn't matter how many features the Outlook developers can come up with. They are still limited because they're only just the Outlook developers. The rest of the world has ideas, too.

When you think of programs as filters, you tend to write software that remains open to enhancement, not only by you and your company but by others who may have a different view of things than you do. In this way, your work is leveraged by others, just as you get to leverage their work.

This brings us to the end of the chapter on Microsoft Windows. But before we move on to the chapter about open systems, I'd like to leave you with a closing thought.

We've looked at the effect that the herd has on the computer industry. As of this writing, the herd is clearly riding the Microsoft bandwagon. Just as there once was a time that "no one was ever fired for buying IBM," today one can maintain one's job security (for a little while longer anyway) by joining the army of individuals recommending a Microsoft solution. But whereas some of the Microsoft software is actually quite good—and I am not afraid to admit that—it is software produced by one company and a select few of those others whom Microsoft considers its allies, if there can be such a thing. There are other developers, other companies, and other voices, all of which deserve a chance to display their creativity.

Despite the overwhelming influence of Microsoft's marketing juggernaut, Microsoft's voice is not the only one in the world of computing. Just because there is an army of people saying that Microsoft Windows is the right approach to computing doesn't mean that it's true. I can go out and get an army that says otherwise.

The soldiers in my army look like a bunch of penguins. They wear red hats and yellow stars. They adapt like chameleons. They speak a strange language with words like "grep," "awk," and "sed."

And they believe in a philosophy called Unix.

A Cathedral? How Bizarre!

First they ignore you. Then they ridicule you. Then they fight you. And then you win.
Gandhi

When the Rolling Stones released their *Forty Licks* CD on October 1, 2002, everyone thought it would go straight to the top of the charts over the following week. It almost did. It made it to the number-two spot. The Stones confirmed that, indeed, you can't always get what you want. This quintessential greatest-hits collection by the Greatest Rock Band of All Time surrendered the number-one spot because the listening public couldn't help falling in love with another collection of greatest hits by no one other than Elvis Aaron Presley, released on September 24, 2002, and modestly titled *ELV1S 30 #1 Hits*[1].

Suspicious minds wanted to know how an old hound dog like Elvis could prevent the Stones from getting their satisfaction. How was it that they couldn't get him off of their cloud? Why were the Stones under Elvis's thumb, instead of the other way around?

The answer is simple. The Stones' music was done in a cathedral, while Elvis borrowed his music from the bazaar of American music. *Huh?* Before you go having your nineteenth nervous breakdown over this one, let me explain. Maybe you'll see why the Stones, instead of Elvis, were crying in the chapel.

Since the early days—back when time was on their side—Mick Jagger and Keith Richards spent many nights together, penning hit after hit that blew our noses and our minds like a, well, you get the idea. It was only rock and roll, but we liked it. Jagger and Richards seemed to be incapable of anything else. They did one thing, and they did it well.

For all their creative genius, however, their work was a closed-source, proprietary kind of effort. Rarely, if ever, did you hear songs by the Stones that came about as a result of collaboration with third parties. Wild horses couldn't pull them out of the cathedral of their minds and into the maelstrom of open-source cooperation. They were victims of their own NIH.

Meanwhile, the wonder of Elvis was that he operated in a bazaar fashion. He liked things all shook up, and his musical styles ran the gamut from rock and roll to blues, country, gospel, ballads, and show tunes, depending on what his latest flame was at the time. His good-luck charm was his versatility. It didn't matter whether it was on the big screen, in front of a studio microphone, or on the famous Ed Sullivan television show—Elvis had a burning love to perform … everything.

---

1.   No, "ELV1S" is not a typo. The fourth letter really is a "1" in the CD name.

Elvis was also a master of reuse. While Mick Jagger and Keith Richards were busy writing good songs, Elvis was busy *borrowing* them—borrowing them and turning them into hits, that is. While he could have written many of the songs he performed, he chose instead to leverage the work of other song-writers in addition to his own. That allowed him to have a much greater impact on the entertainment world. Yes, he became very wealthy from the sales of his music and merchandise. But many others also shared in his good fortune. That's what happens in a true open-source collaborative kind of environment. Everyone benefits.

The King is dead. Long live the King.

Some might say that this comparison of the Rolling Stones and Elvis to Eric Raymond's *The Cathedral and the Bazaar*[2] is a bit of a stretch. After all, the closest Elvis ever got to a bazaar was probably the Memphis Flea Market out on Maxwell Boulevard. And the least likely place to find the producers of *Goat's Head Soup* would be a cathedral. So let's take a look at a real cathedral, or rather a language once found in cathedrals: Latin.

Latin once held the place that English holds today. Through the conquests of Rome, Latin usage had steadily grown from about 250 B.C. until the 6th century. Around that time, the Roman Catholic Church pronounced that Latin was *the* language for scientific, philosophical, and religious writing. So, from that point forward, if you wanted to be a cool priest or scholar, you had to speak Latin. However, with the gradual decline of the Roman Empire, invading barbarians, who, because of their war-like nature had little interest in being intellectually stylish, usually modified Latin to their liking. In adding their own idioms for kill, maim, and plunder, they felt it was their God-given right to subdue the language as well. Meanwhile, the priests and the scholars decried this pollution of their beloved Latin, further continuing to promulgate its importance to an ever-shrinking religious minority, until such time as the only ones who could speak and write Latin did so in the quiet seclusion of cathedrals.

On the other hand, English grew to become the international language not because it was pure or holy, but because it was adaptive. It would admit the entrance of practically any foreign word or concept into its everyday usage. It was able to *interface* with other cultures better than any other language to date. And interface it did. In the wild diversity of the bazaar we call life, Eng-

---

2.   Raymond, Eric S., *The Cathedral and the Bazaar: Musings on Linux and Open Source by an Accidental Revolutionary*. Sebastopol, CA: O'Reilly & Associates, Inc., 2001.

lish found its place among the largest number of nations primarily because of its ability to connect to and with anything.

This is precisely why open-source software (OSS) flourishes. It can be used by anyone to connect anything to anything else. It does this because of its openness: open standards, open protocols, open file formats, open everything. Nothing is hidden in the OSS world. This openness makes it possible for software developers to see how their predecessors did things. If they like what was done before them and can use it, that's great. They have found a useful tool and saved themselves some time. If not, they're at least free to view past mistakes and improve them.

Meanwhile, those software developers who toil away in the cathedrals developing "superior" software eventually find their markets overtaken by works of the open-source developers. Why? Because cathedral-style software developers only develop programs for others who live in the same cathedral. Whether this cathedral is a single company, a single community, or a single nation, sooner or later the software must interface with software outside the cathedral, or else it will surely die.

Adherents of the Unix philosophy and especially today's Linux developers are acutely aware of this. For example, Linux systems sharing a mixed environment with Windows systems often run Samba, a Windows-compatible file-sharing application that is compatible with Windows SMB networking. The irony is that, according to one benchmark, Linux actually outperforms Windows 2000 running Microsoft's own SMB networking.[3]

Most Linux distributions come with the ability to access Windows file systems on other disk partitions. Can Windows perform the reverse? Can Windows access Linux file systems on other partitions? No. Windows is a closed-source, proprietary system that, like the perennial ostrich with its head in the sand, wants to pretend that other file systems don't exist.

By now you probably perceive some similarity between OSS and software that adheres to the Unix philosophy. By themselves, many works of OSS look like small potatoes compared to the larger "industrial-strength" (as some believe) closed-source proprietary software applications. After all, these works are typically produced by lone individuals, at least in the early stages. As a result, these early efforts are typically small projects, lacking in marketing-style

---

3.   John Terpstra, "Using the SNIA CIFS Benchmark Client to Test Samba Performance", CIFS 2002 Conference Proceedings, Santa Clara, CA

flash, but full of substance. But that's okay. Remember that in the Unix world, *small is beautiful*.

Eric Raymond referred to these works as software that "scratches a programmer's personal itch." What appears to be a common goal of many OSS developers is that they just want to get it written. Their backs are often against the wall because of their daily job pressures, and they don't have much time for frills. So, they usually skip most of the fancy glittery stuff that the marketing droids love and, instead, *do one thing well*, which is to produce a lean, mean application that solves a personal need. In the case of the successful ones, these bare-bones solutions strike the matches that set others' imaginations on fire. That is how the hit OSS applications are born.

Once the fire is lit, other members of the OSS development community at large begin to contribute to the program. At first, the program will attract a small, but loyal, following. Then, eventually the software takes on a life of its own, and it grows beyond the scope of its original intent. During this time, dozens of programmers evolve this first system into a larger, more encompassing second system. As of this writing, Linux itself is in the second system phase. A merry time is being had by all.

Obviously, if one wants to strike the match that turns a one-person OSS project into a software phenomenon, one must *build a prototype as soon as possible*. It's not enough simply to talk about a great idea for a piece of software. In the open-source world, those who gain the most respect are those who write the initial version of the software or contribute something of significance later on.[4]

In order for an OSS project to entice the greatest number of users, it must be available on the largest number of platforms. So good OSS developers *choose portability over efficiency*. A program that takes advantage of specific hardware features on a particular machine will not develop as large a following as one that can be run by anyone on his or her favorite platform. By moving away from closed, proprietary architectures and toward open ones, a program can maximize its market potential by addressing the largest number of target platforms.

Consider Microsoft's Internet Explorer Web browser and its competitor from the open-source world, Mozilla. As of this writing, Internet Explorer has a larger market share than Mozilla, mainly because it is the dominant browser

---

4.   This is not meant to discredit those visionaries who act as catalysts in the open-source community. Good ideas have to come from somewhere, and some of these individuals are veritable fountains of originality.

on Microsoft Windows. Windows currently owns the largest share of the desktop market. Mozilla, on the other hand, runs on Windows as well as virtually every Linux and Unix platform out there. As users begin to cut through the Internet Explorer marketing hype and realize what a fine browser Mozilla is, more and more of them on all platforms will switch to Mozilla. Meanwhile, Internet Explorer has barely grown beyond the Windows-installed user base because it lacks the portability to make porting it to other systems inexpensive. If Mozilla succeeds at capturing even half of the Windows-installed base, then it will have won the competition. Any portable browser good enough to capture the hearts and minds of half of the Windows user base would likely capture most of the Linux user base as well.[5]

In order for OSS programs and interfaces to be ported to other platforms easily, it helps to *store data in flat text files*. This kind of openness exposes the file formats to the rest of the world and encourages healthy debate over their contents. This debate ultimately results in open standards for data transmission and storage that are far more ubiquitous than closed-source, proprietary standards.

A good example of this approach is that taken by the folks at OpenOffice.org. They opted for XML as a file format, an excellent choice. XML is a superset of HTML, the language used in Web browsers to display text, tables, and such. XML files are flat text files in that they can be edited with a regular text editor (not a word processor) such as vi or Windows Notepad. As an industry standard, XML may possibly be the best choice for structured interoperable data, not only in flat text files, but also in flat network messages as well. Undoubtedly, the format will evolve over time. As more and more eyes view the data files, the errors and omissions in the format will become evident. This will strengthen and refine the format, as it eventually becomes better than any closed-source format for document storage currently available.

OpenOffice.org's use of flat text files is nothing new, of course. Office suites in the real world have *always* used flat text. Business correspondence is normally carried out on 20-pound white paper transmitted in Number 10 business envelopes. These documents are

- *Portable:* The envelope can be carried down the hall or across the world. Scaleable mechanisms exist for moving documents from place to place, individually and in large groups.

---

5.   See http://www.planettribes.com/allyourbase/

- *Accessible:* Anyone can open the envelope. You don't need a special proprietary tool purchased at great expense from a single vendor to view the contents.

- *Searchable:* Documents can be indexed and placed in file cabinets according to whatever scheme the recipient desires. They can be retrieved in random-access or sequential fashion. The entire text can be searched, albeit slowly.

- *Resilient:* Documents can be stored and retrieved thousands of times, today and in the future. One does not need either to upgrade one's office suite to read the newest documents or to install an older version in order to view a ten-year-old document.

No, we're not suggesting that you abandon your computer and go back to using paper. Paper is still a death certificate for your data, for reasons mentioned elsewhere in this book. However, there is another kind of death that threatens your data: closed-source, proprietary file formats. When your data is stored in non-human-readable file formats owned by a single vendor, then your data is at enormous risk, as Peruvian congressman Dr. Edgar David Villanueva Nuñez pointed out accurately in a letter to Microsoft[6]:

> The use of proprietary systems and formats will make the State ever more dependent on specific suppliers. Once a policy of using free software has been established (which certainly, does imply some cost) then on the contrary migration from one system to another becomes very simple, since all data is stored in open formats.

Open-source programs demand open data formats.

As OSS developers release their software for public consumption, *they use software leverage to their advantage.* This leverage works both ways. First, the developers can use bits and pieces of other OSS projects in their projects. This saves overall development time and helps keep development costs low. Second, the release of good OSS into the world usually attracts other developers, who can leverage that work for their own purposes. Some of this work may eventually find its way back into the original work. Give unto others, and it shall be given unto you.[7]

---

6.   http://www.opensource.org/docs/peru_and_ms.php

7.   Luke 6:38: "Give, and it will be given to you: a good measure, pressed down, shaken together, running over, will be poured into your lap. For the measure you use will be the measure you receive."

One way to improve the chances of success within an OSS project is to *use scripts to increase leverage and portability*. While there are plenty of hard-core low-level coders out there, there is a growing number of people who don't have the time or the chutzpah to work at the lowest levels. By providing an interface to a popular scripting language or two, it is possible to enhance the usefulness of any piece of software dramatically.

If these interfaces gain enough popularity, a significant subcommunity within the OSS community will form. These subcommunities are passionately devoted to experimenting with and extending such interfaces. They will hold user-group meetings and conferences, post to online mailing lists, and generally become the focal point for the greater part of activity surrounding a popular interface.

A couple of examples of this are the communities surrounding Perl and the Concurrent Versions System (CVS) for software version control. CVS has attracted quite a following within the OSS community. Because virtually all of the CVS commands can be used within scripts, numerous tools and add-ons have sprung up to combine them in new and interesting ways. The original authors of CVS would certainly not have predicted many of these uses.

CVS, by design, *avoids CUIs*. Every CVS command can be run from the command line by passing in the appropriate parameters. This has helped make it easier for CVS add-ons to spring up. The basic CVS commands, such as *checkout*, *update*, and *commit*, form the basis of many of the integrated tools built to enhance CVS. The various add-on tools created using these commands often have CUIs. But the basic CVS commands do not. This is one of the main reasons that CVS has flourished.

Perl has gained massive notoriety as an open-source scripting tool. More powerful than the common Unix shells, such as the Bourne and Korn shells, it excels at interfacing with other software. *Nearly all Perl programs act as filters*. In fact, its full name, Practical Extraction Reporting Language, attests that Perl was designed for that purpose. When a program extracts information from someplace, modifies it, and reports it (i.e., "outputs" it), it is fulfilling the role of a filter.

Perl's acceptance also grew because of its extensibility, too. Hackers (in the good sense of the word) found a veritable playground in this "kitchen sink" of languages and proceeded to add libraries to adapt it to a wide variety of situations. Today you can find a Perl module to handle anything from complex mathematics to database development to CGI scripting for the World Wide Web.

Not surprisingly, Perl is a shining example of the "worse is better" lesser tenet of the Unix philosophy—and stunning proof that that which is worse (e.g., Perl) usually has better survivability characteristics than that which is better (e.g., Smalltalk). Few people would contest the notion that Perl is a quirky language with a hideous syntax. And fewer still would suggest that Perl is anything less than rampantly successful.

It should be evident to the reader at this point that OSS more often than not adheres to the Unix philosophy. OSS lends itself to the "bazaar" style of development, a style that Unix developers in the early days coddled and today's Linux developers enthusiastically embrace. But while the Unix philosophy focuses on the design approach, much of the rhetoric coming from the open-source community highlights the software development process. The Unix philosophy combined with open-source development processes is a marriage made in heaven, to use an old cliché. They augment and complement each other nicely.

One area in which the open-source community has made significant advances is marketing. In today's fiercely competitive computing world, it is not enough to produce high-quality software in accordance with sound design principles. One must tell people that one has done so. You can have the best frazzlefloozle in the world, but if no one knows about your frazzlefloozle, it won't matter how good it is. It will fade into obscurity or languish as an undiscovered relic for years.

Many excellent Unix programs have disappeared due to a lack of solid marketing. I could name several of them, if I could only remember them. Get the point?

Microsoft has well understood the value of solid marketing, perhaps better than any other company to date. This is the primary reason why the company has been so successful. Microsoft has produced a number of hit applications, but its strength lies mainly in its ability to convince everyone that its software is the finest on the planet, regardless of quality.

The main issue I have with Microsoft software is that it is developed cathedral-fashion in a closed-source environment. Microsoft has some very talented people who have written some very good software. But Microsoft has not cornered the globe on technological innovation. There are plenty of talented people in the rest of the world who do not work for Microsoft and who write some very good software as well. Because of their cathedral style of development, the Microsoft developers have isolated themselves from the others.

They cannot fully benefit from software leverage because they are not sharing anything that others can augment and give back to them. So, most Windows operating system innovation is undertaken by the Microsoft developers and is thereby limited by their vision. Open-source developers, on the other hand, have the much larger open-source development community to draw from for ideas. In terms of sheer size, the open-source development community dwarfs Microsoft's internal development community. And that—Microsoft's superb marketing efforts notwithstanding—will ultimately be Microsoft's downfall.

At the time of this writing, the Linux development community (rumored to be more than a million developers strong) began to invade the desktop environment, long thought to be Microsoft's stronghold and considered impenetrable by any outsider. In as little as 18 months, the developers of Gnome, a Windows-like application environment popular on Linux, had taken Linux from a Unix command-line user interface to one having nearly as much capability as Windows 95. It took Microsoft more than five years to accomplish the equivalent in going from MS-DOS to Windows 3.1 to Windows 95.

It's hard to see how Microsoft can keep up with this rate of innovation. It is simply outgunned. The KDE community, which may be even larger than the Gnome community, has already been shown to be quite capable of producing commercial-quality GUI software for the desktop environment. Unless Microsoft reinvents itself to meet this challenge, it is only a matter of time before Microsoft's Windows operating system becomes the next OpenVMS (i.e., great software made by a great *little* team).

Microsoft had ignored Linux and the open-source community for nearly a decade. Then, they ridiculed Linux, saying that it was "only a server system" and that it was not suitable for the desktop. Now Microsoft has an all-out desktop war on its hands, with KDE's minions leading the charge.

Was Gandhi right? The market will decide.

Before closing this chapter, it's important that we address one aspect of living and computing in the postmodern era that has been on everyone's mind since the September 11, 2001, attacks on the World Trade Center and the Pentagon: security.

Security has been on everyone's mind in one way or another as a result of that day. This collective security consciousness has also been on the minds of computer scientists as well. And perhaps, in a strange way, the Unix philosophy and open source hold the key to the solution.

In the world of information security and encryption technology, it has long been thought by some people that in order to provide the highest level of security, one must hide everything and batten down the hatches, as it were. The early Unix developers had a different approach. Rather than hide the password data and the algorithm used to encrypt the passwords, they chose instead to make the encrypted passwords and the encryption algorithm plainly visible to anyone and everyone. Anyone was free to attempt to crack the Unix encryption algorithm and was given all the tools to do so. In the spirit of cooperation, those who found ways to crack the Unix password file submitted their solutions to the original developers who in turn incorporated those solutions in future versions of the encryption algorithms. Over the years, after repeated attempts to defeat the Unix password mechanism, some of which were successful, Unix grew to be a far securer system than the original developers were capable of producing without the help of others.

Meanwhile, attempts to achieve security through obscurity in closed-source systems have failed miserably. Security holes in systems such as Windows NT can only be patched as fast as Microsoft, which maintains a tight grip on the source code, can plug them.

In one sense, security is a numbers game, and the numbers don't look very good for closed-source systems. For every malicious hacker (one of the bad guys) out there, there are probably 100 times or even 1,000 times as many good guys. The problem is, the closed-source company can only afford to hire 10 of the good guys to look at their proprietary source code. Meanwhile, in open-source land, 1,000 times as many good guys than the bad guys can look at the source code to resolve security problems. The closed-source companies, no matter how large they are and how much they're willing to spend, simply cannot keep up with the number of good guys in the open-source community at large.

The implications for open-source software versus closed-source proprietary software here are significant. With many more eyes looking at the security mechanisms in OSS, OSS will eventually prove the more secure of the two. Furthermore, as individuals, companies, and nations become increasingly aware of the need to audit the software used for information security, it will become evident that the only security software that can be trusted is one for which you have the source code.

At some point, everyone must decide whether to trust the producer of the software used to protect information. Everyone has to make his or her own moral and ethical judgment of the software's provider. Can that provider truly be trusted? When your finances, reputation, or physical or national security are at stake, the only acceptable solution is one that lets you verify the software down to the very last line of code.

In the world in which we live, there are both open and closed societies. The closed societies operate much like the cathedral development environment, where the source code is kept under wraps by a privileged few who decide what to leave in and what to leave out. New ideas spread slowly in those societies. And the development of effective security mechanisms that keep pace with the introduction of new threats can take years.

The open societies of this world, like the OSS community, are seemingly chaotic, but also brashly imaginative. Creativity abounds. Ideas for new technology, especially security technology, emerge at a frenetic pace. Open societies' ability to respond rapidly with innovative ideas ensures that no threat can remain a threat for long. Like the developers of the Unix password algorithm, their willingness to remain vulnerable will ultimately lead them to the greatest levels of security.

12

Brave New (Unix) World

A map of the world that does not include Utopia is not worth even glancing at.
—Oscar Wilde

If you listen to the marketing messages of most software companies today, you will find that each espouses its own particular path to software utopia: "Our solutions integrate systems"; "Our process accelerates the development cycle"; "Our graphical user interface gets you going quickly"; "Run your database applications at lower cost." There is no doubt that they have spent countless hours and mountains of dollars rationalizing their approaches. They make their arguments sound pretty convincing. And many of them have killed more trees getting their messages out than we've bulldozed to make room for housing.

I'm no oracle, but I have made a simple observation. The Unix operating system and its concomitant philosophy have been around for more than 25 years. In an industry where the pace of innovation is constantly accelerating, it is most unusual that a single approach to system design and software architecture has endured for so long. Not only has it weathered the storms of thousands or perhaps millions of critics, it continues to thrive and is still gaining ground today. In fact, as the latest incarnation of Unix, Linux stands to overwhelm the world's largest software monopoly in the near future.

About every 10 years or so, a major paradigm shift has hit the computer world. In the early 1960s, mainframe computing was staunchly entrenched in computer labs everywhere. Then, in the 1970s minicomputers and time-sharing engendered the golden age of third-generation hardware. The 1980s saw the advent of the graphical user interface and planted the notion that people might consider a computer a personal thing. In the 1990s, we saw the commoditization of personal computers and the rise of global networking with the Internet and the World Wide Web. In the new millennium, we are experiencing mass decentralization, mass customization, and even unprecedented cooperation with an industry phenomenon known as "open source."

Interestingly, Unix has not only been a part of those paradigm shifts, it has usually acted as a catalyst for most of them. Beginning with the minicomputer, Unix spread (some might say, like a cancer!) throughout the computing world. The X Window System, developed on Unix, was the first graphical application platform that caught on in a big way. The Apache Web server, first run on Unix, grew to become the leading Web server on the Internet. The appeal of Linux, an unencumbered implementation of Unix for the personal computer, has mobilized a massive army of programmers intent on making all important software applications freely available to everyone.

Each of these paradigm shifts has created waves of opportunity for resourceful individuals and companies that realize early on that things are changing fundamentally. Those that sense the paradigm shift earliest often stand to ride the wave the best. The Unix adherents of yesteryear and the Linux advocates of today were and are open to these world-shaking transformations.

Despite the fact that Unix and its philosophical adherents have always been on the cutting edge when major technological advances occur, some would claim that Unix and even Linux are stale, worn-out technologies that went out with the minicomputers of yesteryear. It's a brave new world out there, they say. It's a GUI world. It's a networked world. It's a commodity world.[1] It's a wireless world.

It's a Unix world, really. Because Unix has demonstrated time and again its amazing ability to adapt to whatever comes along. When people said it was too expensive to run on anything but business servers, Linus Torvalds's Linux[2] proved them wrong. When people said that it would never compete with Microsoft Windows on the desktop, the Linux-based KDE developers saw this as a challenge. And—this one's my personal favorite—today, while many people consider Windows to be a better game platform than Linux, I would point out that people were running games on Unix long before game pioneer Atari sold its first game console.

So as the technology race continues, the Unix philosophy will continue to be a driving force, not only in operating-system design, but in other areas of innovation as well. In this chapter, we're going to look at how the Unix philosophy has made its way into other projects, technologies, methodologies, and design approaches. Many of these technologies claim to bring about a kind of nirvana or a subset of a software utopia. That's fine. It's okay for them to make these kinds of claims if that will get them noticed. At least we become aware of them that way. Many of these efforts are full of very good ideas. My only regret is that I cannot participate in all of them, for each holds a particular

1.   As of this writing, you can purchase a 1.1-GHz personal computer running a version of Linux from Walmart.com for less than USD $200. The Windows version is slightly more expensive. Of course, by the time you read this, you're probably thinking that system is overpriced. That's okay. As we've said before, next year's machine will be faster. And cheaper, too!

2.   Unix even adapted by changing its name to Linux because the market perceived that Unix was too old to make it in the postmodern computing era. But everyone knows that Linux is simply the latest implementation of the Unix philosophy.

fascination for me either because of what they have accomplished or what they promise.

To make it easier to identify those tenets of the Unix philosophy that apply to a particular endeavor, you can refer to Table 12.1 for a list of acronyms used throughout the rest of this chapter. The major tenets are in caps and the lesser tenets are in lower case.

Most of these technologies also have a primary theme or overriding concept, which I will highlight at the beginning of the discussion of each.

Table 12.1   *Acronyms Used in Chapter 12*

SMALL	Small is beautiful.
1THING	Make each program do one thing well.
PROTO	Prototype early, as in "as soon as possible."
PORT	Choose portability over efficiency.
FLAT	Store data in flat ASCII files.
REUSE	Use software leverage to your advantage.
SCRIPT	Use scripts whenever possible.
NOCUI	Avoid captive user interfaces.
FILTER	Make every program a filter.
custom	Allow the user to tailor his or her environment.
kernel	Make operating system kernels small.
lcase	Use lowercase and keep it short.
trees	Save trees.
silence	Silence is golden.
parallel	Think parallel.
sum	The sum of the parts is greater than the whole.
90cent	Look for the 90-percent solution.
worse	Worse is better.
hier	Think hierarchically.

Java

Tenets: PORT, FLAT, REUSE, trees, parallel, hier
Central concept: Choose portability over efficiency.

Sun Microsystems' Java programming language has been a phenomenon in its own right. As the heir apparent to the portable-language-of-choice throne once held by the C programming language, it has firmly established itself as the de facto language for new application development today. It isn't perfect, and it has its quirks. Yet, it is rapidly being adopted by the application programming masses.

Sun's promotional message, "write once, run anywhere," speaks resoundingly of the value of portability. And while Java is more portable than C, it is only about 95 percent as efficient. Given the aforementioned advantages of Java's portability, however, it's difficult to understand why anyone would worry about the 5 percent loss in efficiency.

Still, old habits die hard. For those purists who insist on wringing every last bit of performance out of the hardware, C is still the language of choice, as it is for many Linux developers, especially those working on the Linux kernel. That's okay. Comparatively speaking, only a handful of people actually work on the kernel. The largest group of developers by far comprises those cranking out applications to run on Linux and Windows platforms. For them, Java fits the bill quite nicely.

In promoting Java as an open standard, Sun has done a reasonable job of walking a fine line between proprietary control and open-source flexibility. Many developers question Sun's motives for retaining strong control over Java's fate and would prefer that the evolution of Java be managed by a publicly accessible open-standards body. But we'll leave those issues to the marketers and strategists and instead focus on the technical and philosophical aspects of the language.

Code reuse is very popular among Java programmers, largely due to its object-oriented architecture. Through hierarchical inheritance mechanisms, most Java classes take advantage of code written by someone else in the inheritance chain. New classes are often extensions of existing classes. Sun's marketing notwithstanding, this ease of reuse has caused Java to gain rapid, widespread acceptance.

Java adheres to the Unix philosophy tenet of flat-file usage with its property file mechanism. Whereas in some application environments the configuration information is stored in binary files, Java property files are ostensibly human-readable. Text search engines on a system can also index them, making it easy for developers to locate any property in an environment in a moment.

Java does more than pay lip service to parallel operations. Its core classes include a set of objects for creating and manipulating threads. Hence, many Java applications written today are multithreaded. This is not always a good thing, as some developers have found plenty of ways to abuse this mechanism. But in general it has served the Java community well.

Another step in the right direction is Sun's Javadoc. This tool generates API documentation in HTML format from the comments in the source code. Since the output is HTML, most Javadoc documentation is viewed using a Web browser, rather than by printing the documents themselves. We're saving forests by the hectare here.

With all of the things that Java does right, is there anything that Java does wrong? Of course. While C had the dreaded *#include* directive that was responsible for endless name collisions between variables, Java has found a way to reinvent this nightmare with its classpath mechanism. Time and again, we see programmers struggling with the same kinds of issues with classpaths as the C programmers did with the *#include* directive. Maybe someone will invent a solution to this problem someday. In the meantime, we're stuck with it.

Finally, the issue of who controls Java keeps rearing its ugly head from time to time. Many hardcore Linux developers eschew Java because it isn't open source in the way that they think that open source ought to be. This kind of thinking may be too restrictive. Sun Microsystems acts as a kind of benevolent dictator with respect to Java. It makes the sources available to anyone who wants them. It responds to suggestions and criticism. It simply wants to retain some measure of control over them to be sure that they are not polluted or absconded with by another entity.

That other entity is Microsoft. Sun is playing a life-or-death chess match with Microsoft, struggling to wrest control of the development environment from the software behemoth. Meanwhile, Microsoft has attempted to upset the Java juggernaut with the introduction of .Net and its own C# programming language. Will Java survive the onslaught of these? Most likely it will. Java is perceived as being more portable than anything that comes out of Redmond, regardless of the marketing hype. And there is a large community of developers who believe that portability is more than marginally useful.

Object-Oriented Programming

Tenets: SMALL, 1THING, REUSE, hier
Central concept: Use software leverage to your advantage.

After the discussion on Java, you may be wondering why we're bringing up the idea of object-oriented programming (OOP). The reason is that, while Java is the leading object-oriented language today, it is not the whole story about OOP. And—surprise of surprises—some programmers have demonstrated that one can write non-object-oriented programs in Java if one chooses to do so. (To one's peril, I might add.)

OOP represents a tectonic shift from structured or procedural programming, the way things were done in languages like C and Pascal. This kind of shift comes along every 10 to 15 years in the computer field. When it does, it changes the way we look at everything. It acts as a driving force for the development of tons of software to implement the new paradigm. It usually engenders the rewriting of lots of old software that shines in unexpected, interesting ways under the new architecture.

OOP fits in well with the Unix philosophy. While some functions in procedural languages often consume a page or more, well-written objects in the OOP style usually lean toward smaller sizes. Hence, OOP is an embodiment of the small-is-beautiful tenet. In fact, those programmers who have a good grasp of the Unix philosophy make the best OOP developers. They understand the intrinsic value of small tools that interface well with others.

On the down side, however, one can easily imagine a gazillion reusable classes, each written by a programmer suffering from the NIH syndrome, each an extension of an extension of an existing class somewhere. This is occurring at a fast pace because OOP is entering its Second System phase, where everyone and his brother and his Uncle Ned back on the farm is writing object-oriented code. One can only hope that the Second System phase of OOP will be a mercifully short one.

Ostensibly, good OOP systems consist of a large collection of small objects, each having a single functional intent, organized hierarchically, and highly integrated. That is the essence of OOP. Done well, a system of this sort can be highly efficient. Like the procedural architectures of yesteryear, the OOP concept can be abused, and the relationship graph of a set of objects can look less like a tree and more like a bowl of spaghetti. And sometimes programmers build OO mansions when OO shacks or even OO outhouses are called for. The cure for this situation is *refactoring*, a process whereby code paths and object relationships are analyzed to reduce complexity. OOP is here to stay ... at least until the next tectonic shift comes along.

Extreme Programming

Tenets: SMALL, 1THING, PROTO, custom, sum, 90cent
Central concept: Build a prototype early and work iteratively with your customer.

If you'll take a look at the definition of extreme programming (XP) at http://www.extremeprogramming.org/what.html, you might think that the inventors of XP have usurped the Unix philosophy, slapped a new label on it, and called it their own. And you may be right. If anything, the XP methodology affirms what the Unix developers of yesterday and the Linux developers of today have been saying all along: Build a prototype. Do it now. Don't wait.

To their credit, the XP community has done a great service in formalizing iterative development and communicating its value to the nontechnical management and executive individuals of the world. They have taken much of what the Unix programmers have been saying all along and made it palatable to people who live in the worlds of accounting and marketing spin. They are busy teaching them that the best way to develop software may be to sit down, try it out, and then talk to the programmer about what you like or don't like about it. Hurrah!

One area of focus where the XP thinkers have brought clarity is testing. Unix adherents have usually tested their software by releasing early prototypes to willing guinea pigs hungry to get their hands on the latest anything. While this has served the Unix community well as the number of testers is usually large under these circumstances, it occasionally leaves gaps. The XP approach, on the other hand, is to write the test software first. This helps you nail down the software's business requirements early, they say.

In practice, early testing in the XP methodology is a mixed blessing. It is good to involve the customers early in the testing. Sometimes developers will get so bogged down in writing the tests early on, however, that they do not pay enough attention to what the customer is asking for. Even worse, as the requirements evolve over time, one usually has to go back and rework the tests, something that doesn't always get done during the frantic period approaching the end of a software development project. When carried to the extreme (no pun intended here), this approach assumes one had better know all of the requirements up front because one is going to write the tests for those requirements.

The problem is that there will not be as much time to modify those tests later as the requirements change. It would be far better to spend the time building the prototype first without the tests, get it into the hands of the users, and then write the tests. That way you write fewer unnecessary tests and spend more time getting in tune with what the customer really wants. Then, to raise the overall quality of the application, you write only those tests that give you the biggest bang for your efforts. This is not unlike using a code profiler to determine where the program spends its time, then spending 10 percent of your effort in order to gain a 90 percent improvement.

Despite these differences, I suspect that the Unix community and the XP community are on very good terms. They share a lot of common goals and their approaches are quite similar. XP and Unix are like the United Kingdom and the United States. They share common roots. Both speak the same language. But the Brits are a little more formal. And the Yanks are a little more "cowboy" in their approach.

Refactoring

Tenets: SMALL, 1THING, PROTO, FILTER, 90cent
Central concept: Simplify, simplify.

The interest in refactoring these days is a formalization of what programmers, hackers, and other tinkerers love to do: twiddle with something to make it better. Its chief proponent is probably Martin Fowler, coauthor of the book *Refactoring: Improving the Design of Existing Code.* The fundamental idea behind all refactoring efforts is that it is possible to improve the internal structure of a software system without altering its external behavior.

One cool aspect of refactoring is that it helps you to realize that interfaces are important, perhaps more so than you may have understood them to be in the past. This is crucial when you're talking about a system consisting of a large number of small tools all playing well together. Unless you have defined solid interfaces between them, you end up with a large collection of totally random stuff with no rationale behind it. In other words, you have a mess.

Developers and other philosophers are writing volumes about design patterns and other techniques used in software refactoring today. Alas, people are finally writing about the processes that have been going on inside programmers' heads for years. This kind of analysis can only lead to a better understanding of what we do and a move towards improving what we do.

A common axiom of refactoring is that it should take place in small, incremental changes rather than large rewrites. Here the Unix philosophers and the refactorers share a common ground. Unix developers have worked in a small, incremental, iterative development style. However, like the difference between the XP methodology and the Unix philosophy, the Unix approach rests upon much common ground with the refactorers, yet departs from it in at least one aspect, that of the willingness to "throw stuff away." The refactorers rarely advocate total rewrites of anything. The Unix developers frequently build the First System, throw it away, and then build the Second System, knowing full well that this way is frequently the most expedient path to the Third System (i.e., the correct one). So the Unix developers are a bit bolder in this regard. Sometimes a system is so bad that the quickest way to software utopia is to take a different road altogether.

Many of the decisions one makes in refactoring are efforts to help the software conform to a particular design pattern or to invent a new design pattern if the situation doesn't fit any of the known ones in existence. All design patterns, no matter how eloquent, are simply supersets of the original design pattern; that is, every program is a filter. This is similar to the old adage, it's all ones and zeroes. The most complex numerical or logical system can always be reduced to a series of binary representations.

In refactoring, as one seeks the proper design pattern as a model for one's architecture, it is best then to remember that you probably don't fully understand a program's logical process until you can express it in the form of a filter with a single input and a single output. When you have arrived at that level of understanding, then you are ready to refactor.

The Apache Jakarta Project

Tenets: SMALL, 1THING, PROTO, REUSE, sum
Central concept: Open source cooperation leverages the work of many, yielding great benefits.

When one looks at the level of cooperation, the faithful implementation of standards, the honest technical interaction, and the consistently high quality of the software produced by the Apache Jakarta Project,[3] one can only come to one conclusion: open-source development works.

As evidenced by the way the projects are governed, the way the software is written, and the enthusiastic acceptance of its users, Jakarta has clearly put a stake in the ground that causes all proprietary software developers to sit up and take notice.

What has made the project so successful? No one thing, really. It is the sum of all the parts that make it a powerful, cohesive development organization. But if one had to single out a factor that has had more influence than any other, it would be the idea that community is more important than software. In other words, the democratic cooperation of many minds is better than a closed caste system of developers working for a single (usually corporate) entity.

The Jakarta software is freely available to anyone who wants it. Because of the generally recognized high quality of the software, large corporations have been using it to run critical business functions. The side effect of this is that consultants and developers have sprung up to provide customization services to adapt the software for specific industries. This illustrates an important principle: there is still money to be made from free software.

We have seen that the computing industry has ridden several broad waves of opportunity. First, there was the hardware wave, where much money was invested in the development of new CPUs, memory, and storage devices with sufficient power to get us to the next wave. Large companies like IBM and Digital Equipment Corporation made lots of money during that wave. The second wave, the software wave, saw the likes of Lotus, Novell, and Microsoft rise to the top as they capitalized on the need for software and applications to meet the needs of business. The next wave is one of services, where end users are no longer interested in what's under the covers as long as one can get the desired content when one wants it.

Note that the first two waves ended when the bottom dropped out of the price-performance model of the respective wave. The commoditization of PCs has driven the profits out of hardware. Likewise, free software is making it nearly impossible to make money from selling software anymore. The profitability point now resides at the service end of the spectrum. When everyone can get any piece of software or hardware for a negligible cost, then service

3.   http://jakarta.apache.org.

(largely through customization) becomes the differentiator. As of this writing, this is already occurring with service offerings such as the Red Hat Network and various premium services offered by the media outlets such as CNN and the *New York Times*. We have moved from the mass production of the Industrial Era to the mass customization of the Information Age.

So keep an eye on what happens to the Apache Jakarta Project. It is a microcosm of what's happening to the best of the open-source development community at large.

The Internet

Tenets: REUSE, trees, sum, worse, hier
Central concept: If worse is better, then the plethora of bad Web pages out there guarantees the Net's longevity.

With over three billion Web pages on the Net, the World Wide Web has shown itself to be a veritable beast rising out of the sea of humanity. While promoting the best that humankind has to offer, it also probes the nether depths of depravity. Every time you think that you've seen it all, the Net comes back with a vengeance to make you feel like you're chipping away at an iceberg with a toothpick. With a track record like that, it's likely to be around for a very, very long time.

Reuse is a popular concept on the Web these days. Not only are millions of people illegally sharing and reusing each other's copyrighted music CDs, they're also legally sharing favorite HTML code snippets, graphical images, icons, and JavaScript programs to make their own Web pages. In fact, the nonprogrammer individuals out there are probably better at reusing code than most software developers. It matters little that there is a lot of garbage out there. What counts is that the garbage is freely available to anyone through the feature provided by most Web browsers that allows the user to view the HTML and JavaScript source code. It is as if the Internet is the world's largest dumpster, and half the world has gone dumpster diving.

Of course, the World Wide Web has lots of great content. And text-based search engines make it relatively easy to find. As long as you realize that on the Internet there are at least 10 times as many ax grinders as there are axes to grind, you'll do fine. You may even enjoy grinding a few axes of your own.

The World Wide Web may redeem itself by finally stemming the torrent of paper spewing from printers everywhere. Remember when everyone said that the introduction of computers into the working world would lead to the paperless office? Well, much to everyone's surprise, it was discovered that computers help generate more paper use, not less. But spreading around reams of paper to one's coworkers in the office is not nearly as much fun as flying it on a worldwide flagpole to see which individuals across the globe will salute it. And so the World Wide Web, in eminently practical fashion, may actually fulfill one of the Unix philosophy's lesser tenets by helping us save trees.

Wireless Communications

Tenets: SMALL, PORT, custom, worse
Central concept: Cheap, effective, portable communications make for the next "killer app."

Compared to landline telephones, cell phones aren't very efficient. They make lousy speakerphones. They drop off in the middle of important conversations when you're zipping down the expressway. Their batteries seem to need constant recharging as compared with their semitethered cordless brethren found in the home. But we all know why we love them: portability.

Cell phones are perhaps the best example yet of the value of portability over efficiency. The fidelity of the cell phones isn't the greatest, and yet people find that they are increasingly using them instead of their home phones. People who have problems programming a microwave oven know which buttons to push on their cell phones to bring them into submission. It's not because cell phones are easier to understand than microwaves. They're not. It's just that the need to communicate is so great, apparently even greater than the need to eat.

Cell phones have also pushed the small-is-beautiful tenet of the Unix philosophy to the extreme as well. My first cell phone was a clunker. It weighed as much as a brick. It had mediocre reception outside of the primary coverage areas. It cost a small fortune in phone charges. And it was worth every penny I paid for it. Nowadays ultraslim, ultrasmart phones may be purchased for less than a night out on the town, and many are offered gratis from wireless providers' licensed agents.

What is even more interesting with cell phones and other wireless communications devices is the issue of *convergence*. It is not enough that we use cell phones to talk to one another. We want to be able to do everything with a cell phone that we can do with a home computer. This means sending and receiving live video, playing games, converting spoken messages to email, translating foreign speech on the fly, reading email, accessing the Internet, watching streaming video, and so on.

No, cell phones will not be able to do these things as well as desktop computers. But they will be just good enough. It's the worse-is-better tenet again. That which is cheap and effective is more useful than that which is big and expensive. People will not care that the little screen on their cell phone isn't as large as the one on their laptops. What they want is something good enough that is also *portable*.

Do you doubt that cell phones are up to the task? If you just look at the … er, please excuse me. I have a call coming in.

Web Services

Tenets: SMALL, 1THING, PORT, FLAT, REUSE, filter, sum
Central concept: The Unix philosophy implemented on the network.

It was only a matter of time before everyone realized that Gordon Bell's statement that "the network becomes the system" is absolutely true.[4] Sun Microsystems later popularized this notion with its "the network is the computer" marketing campaign. And while there were some interesting attempts along the way to realize that vision (e.g., CORBA, DCOM), none thus far had showed the promise of turning the network into a gestalt computer like Web services have done thus far.[5]

Web services use a model consisting of a collection of small, network-based components or tools. Simply described, the technology is the summation of HTTP as a transport and Simple Object Access Protocol (SOAP) as a

---

4.   Gordon Bell et. al. "Why Digital Is Committed to Ethernet for the Fifth Generation." New York, February 10, 1982, at http://research.microsoft.com/~gbell/Digital/Ethernet_announcement_820210c.pdf.

5.   See http://www.w3.org/2002/ws. This URL may morph into http://www.w3.org/2003/ws at some point, so you may need to start with http://www.w3.org and look around from there.

messaging language on top of that transport. As you might suspect, its architecture has a lot in common with the Unix philosophy. In an ideal implementation, each Web service

- Does one thing well
- Acts as a filter between messages from the client to the server and vice versa
- Employs flat text in the form of XML for messages
- Is written in a portable language from reusable components

Is it any wonder that Web services are catching on in a big way? Both the open-source community with the DotGNU project[6] and Microsoft with its .NET initiative[7] are implementing frameworks around this technology. The potential that Web services hold for business applications is huge, and it could possibly be the start of the next tectonic shift in the computing world.

Although the Web services technology is inching along as a standard at the World Wide Web Consortium (W3C), the opposing factions implementing that standard are gearing up for a long bloody brouhaha. If the rivalry between Linux and Windows is to be computer Armageddon, then the struggle for dominance in the Web services space will be guerilla warfare. Both sides understand the rules of engagement, and both are showing signs that they may be willing to subvert them.

One of the biggest points of contention in this struggle is and will continue to be security. The Microsoft Passport logon mechanism has already fallen under heavy fire by the research arm of AT&T Labs.[8] Not surprisingly, Microsoft's approach to authentication is based on getting the necessary credentials from a single entity, namely Microsoft. This has raised the ire of the open-source community, which has claimed that no single entity should have the right to hold such credentials.

The issue once again boils down to a matter of trust. In this respect, the open-source advocates have the edge. One cannot completely trust a security mechanism produced by any human organization, entity, or government

6.   See http://www.dotgnu.org.

7.   See http://www.microsoft.com/net.

8.   David P. Kormann and Aviel D. Rubin. "Risks of the Passport Single Signon Protocol," *Computer Networks*, Vol. 33, 2000: 51–58.

unless one can view the source code used to construct that mechanism. Anything else ultimately will lead to control of individuals and, ultimately, human slavery.

The monks in the cathedral respectfully disagree.

Artificial Intelligence

Tenets: PROTO, hier
Central concept: If you build a prototype early enough, you may learn from what the machine tells you.

After reading some of the other discussions in this chapter, you may be wondering why we're taking up the subject of artificial intelligence (AI). After all, isn't AI old boring stuff left to tenured professors and geeks too geeky for mainstream geekhood? Haven't all of the good Sci-Fi books about AI already been written? The AI crowd has been telling us for a very long time that computers are going to be smarter than we are someday. Most of this has been laughed off as a techno dream. Someday is still sometime in the future. The AI community has never really delivered anything of value, save for IBM's Deep Blue[9] and other chess-playing marvels.

I am here to tell you that the AI community will have its day in the sun. It may be sooner than you think. And you may not like it, because when you're dealing with someone or something smarter than you, you may not realize when that someone or something is in control.

First, much of AI theory focuses on the quest for ways to traverse massive decision trees. That's the idea behind the chess-playing programs. The decision tree for the game of chess is a finite, albeit very large, one. Older chess-playing computers could only search decision trees a few plies deep. IBM's Deep Blue used an IBM SP2 32-CPU RS6000 parallel machine with 256 chess accelerator chips to examine 100 million positions per second and perform selective searches up to 30 plies deep.

Remember the idea of next _____'s machine? That's right. Someday we'll have the power of Deep Blue in our wristwatches. I can hardly wait. Then Kasparov will be able to carry Deep Blue everywhere and really figure out why it beat him.

---

9.   See http://www.research.ibm.com/deepblue.

Second, developers have found that in prototyping AI programs early, they occasionally discover that the programs themselves teach them something new. Developing AI software then becomes an iterative process involving not the end user, but the computer itself. Obviously, the more often one does this with progressively faster machines and more intelligent programs, the smarter these programs will become.

Of course, this increase in AI isn't without its perils, as the Sci-Fi authors have reminded us for so long. To see a live example of how this technology can be used for good purposes (at least from a business perspective), visit the Amazon.com site. Notice the number of ways that Amazon tries to persuade you to buy books related to any book you've purchased, any book you've looked at, any book you wished you owned, any book your friends have recommended, any book your mother purchased, any book of yours that your ex-girlfriend burned, any book that your spouse found in your briefcase, any book your dog ate, any book you've read in the bathroom, any book your kid brother borrowed and never returned, and so on.

This kind of AI, one that seeks patterns in human behavior by matching keys between two or more disparate databases, is a relatively new trend. Due to its enormous commercial potential, it will likely gain ground as a hot technology in the coming years as companies seek to maximize their profits. So far, companies like Amazon are exploring the obvious connections between databases. It will get more interesting, however, when AI heuristics begin to point out the not-so-obvious connections. It's fun when Amazon offers you a cool book on Linux-based music composition. It might not be fun when the supermarket has figured out the exact day to raise the price of your favorite coffee.

In this chapter we have looked at several examples of how ideas from the Unix philosophy have infiltrated other technologies. The discussion is by no means comprehensive, and I apologize if I have missed your favorite technology. There are so many fascinating ones out there today that it would have taken yet another book to discuss them. Even then, such a tome would be incomplete, as new technologies come along every day.

My desire is that you will now be able identify those ideas that are Unix-like by nature in any endeavor. As you see the patterns emerge, you will be better equipped to nudge them in the direction of openness and community, rather than seclusion and exclusivity. An idea shared is worth two kept in the mind. We all benefit when one shares one's ideas and we remain open to the ideas of others.

This chapter also serves to illustrate another important point: Unix versions may come and go, but the Unix philosophy will endure for a long time. This is especially true of Linux. Linux will most likely become the version of Unix that fulfills the prediction that Unix will be the world's operating system of choice. Even as Linux overcomes its rivals and enemies through openness and inclusion, Linux may see itself superseded by a newer operating system someday that embodies the Unix philosophy in ways that we couldn't possibly see today. This, too, is okay. When that happens, those who already know how to "think Unix" will be ready for it.

Go forth. Do one thing. Do it well. In the end, what you accomplish will be greater than the sum of all that you do.

About the Author

Mike Gancarz is an applications and programming consultant in Atlanta, Georgia. Using Linux, Unix, and Java tools, his team develops award-winning imaging solutions for the financial services industry.

An expert in Unix application design, Mike has been an advocate of the Unix approach for more than twenty years. As a member of the team that gave birth to the X Window System, he wrote *uwm*, the first customizable window manager for X. Although *uwm* has long been put out to pasture, the usability concepts he pioneered are still found in modern window managers running on Linux today.

While working at Digital Equipment Corporation's Unix Engineering Group in Nashua, New Hampshire, Mike became intimately familiar with the Unix command set in leading the port of the Unix commands and utilities to the 64-bit Alpha processor. His other efforts at Digital led to the development of COMET, a high-performance text retrieval system. Written in the Unix shell language, COMET revolutionized technical support at Digital by indexing most of the company's internal documentation and source code, making instant answers available to Digital's support staff around the world.

Later Mike turned to independent consulting on web development projects in the Atlanta area. His clients have included IBM, Sprint, Worldcom, and various financial services firms.

Mike resides in a northern Atlanta suburb with his wife, two children, and the world's most adorable chihuahua. When he's not tinkering with Linux, he enjoys long games of *Civilization* and an occasional game of chess.

Index